STATUS FORCES IN DELINQUENT BOYS

Martin Gold

Inter-Center Program on Children, Youth, and Family Life
INSTITUTE FOR SOCIAL RESEARCH
The University of Michigan
Ann Arbor, Michigan
1963

The Institute for Social Research of The University of Michigan is engaged in basic and applied research in the social sciences. The Institute has two main research units. The Survey Research Center is concerned with the application of sample survey methods to the study of economic behavior, human relations in organizations, and public attitudes and behavior in relation to public issues. The Research Center for Group Dynamics studies the behavior of people in groups. The research is conducted in industry, education, government and community life as well as in the laboratory, in an effort to discover the determinants of behavior, of group effectiveness and of human satisfactions.

Inquiries regarding the Institute and its research program may be addressed to the Director of the Institute.

To

The Flint Youth Study Staff

1957 - 1960

whose work I report here

INTER-CENTER PROGRAM ON CHILDREN, YOUTH, AND
FAMILY LIFE

MONOGRAPH SERIES:

The Apprehended Delinquent in Flint

ACKNOWLEDGMENTS

This study is the result of the cooperative efforts of the staff of the Flint Youth Study. My authorship of this report merely represents my role as director of this particular effort on the study and my final responsibility for what is written here. I would like to take this opportunity to thank the Flint Youth Study staff and other members of The University of Michigan faculty for their participation in the research process and their constructive comments on the manuscript.

My special thanks go to Dr. Ronald Lippitt and Dr. Stephen Withey, co-directors of the Institute for Social Research Program on Children, Youth, and Family Life, for their active support; Dr. Morris Janowitz, for his advice and encouragement on all phases of this work; Dr. David Bordua, Dr. Dorwin Cartwright, Dr. Guy E. Swanson, and Dr. Robert Vinter, who commented so constructively on the manuscript; Dr. Charles Seashore, for his part in organizing the delinquency rate data and for his cooperation throughout; Mrs. Estelle Antell, Mrs. Margaret B. Simberg, and Mr. Jack Logan, who saw the Flint field office smoothly through the complicated task of data collection; Miss Kathryn Weimar, who kept the data organized through the processing stages and prepared the tables and bibliography; Mr. Shah J. Sharad, Mr. Ronald Calhoun, and Mr. James Swinehart for their aid in data analysis; Mrs. Norma M. Harris, Mrs. Alice Phelps, Miss Shirley Woodcock, and Mrs. Geraldine Preston for their careful preparation of various stages of manuscript; Mr. Lawrence Kersten for sharing his findings on recreational facilities; the workers in the several departments of the Institute for Social Research who coded interviews and prepared data for electronic computation under the supervision of Mrs. Charlotte Winter, Mr. Laurence Wiener, and Mr. John Sonquist; Superintendent of Schools Spencer Myers, Lieutenant Thomas Waldron, and Sergeant Clare Brown for their help in gaining access to data in Flint; the citizens of Flint who served as interviewers on the study, and the Flint parents and boys who contributed their time as sources for data.

M. G.

Ann Arbor, Michigan
February, 1963

PREFACE

This is the second in the series of monographs for professional youth workers and for colleagues in social research reporting the field research activities of the Flint Youth Study.

The purpose of this program has been to investigate with a social psychological perspective the phenomena of behavioral deviancy in the processes of youth development, and to collaborate with community leaders in utilizing the research findings to develop and evaluate program experiments derived from research and theory and aimed at improving some aspect of the socialization or re-socialization of youth.

The resources of the Institute for Social Research have been mobilized in this joint program of the Survey Research Center and the Research Center for Group Dynamics. The financial support for this community research continuity has been provided by the National Institute of Mental Health (Grant MH 09109), with continuing consultation by Dr. Raymond Gould of the Professional Service Branch of NIMH.

The indispensible linkage with community settings, and continuing guidance in the research utilization process has been provided by the Flint Youth Study Policy Board consisting of:

Mr. Peter Clancy, Assistant Director, Mott Program (Chairman)
Lt. Tom Waldron, Juvenile Division, Flint Police Department (Vice-Chairman)
Mr. Jack Logan, Flint Youth Study Field Director, (Executive Secretary)
Mr. Craig Berke, Associate Secretary of the Council of Social Agencies
Dr. William Carroll, Department of Sociology, Flint Community Junior College
Dr. George Chamis, Educational Services, Flint Schools
Mr. Ted Cobb, Executive Secretary, Urban League
Mr. Lester Ehrbright, Pupil Personnel Director, Flint Schools
Mr. Maurice Frost, Assistant Superintendent, Flint Public Schools
Dr. Paul Jordan, Director, Flint Child Guidance Clinic
Dr. Ronald Lippitt, Institute for Social Research, University of Michigan
Mr. William Lucas, Flint Fire Department and Labor Council
Mr. Robert Potter, Department of Sociology, University of Michigan, Flint

Rev. Mr. Earle Ramsdell, Greater Flint Council of Churches
Mr. James Randall, Department of Sociology, Flint Community Jr.
　College
Mr. Joseph Rider, Director, Big Brothers of Greater Flint
Mr. Donald Sinn, Director of Recreation and Parks Board
Judge George Stevens, Juvenile Division, Probate Court

The study by Dr. Martin Gold, reported in this volume, is one of the six basic field research studies which have preceded the second phase of research utilization designs. Dr. Gold's study of a matched sample of delinquent and non-delinquent boys and their parents, from blue collar and white collar families, is focused on the theoretical problem of linking the phenomena of social class (e.g., economic and occupational status) to the community, the educational system and interpersonal processes in the family and to the attitudinal and behavioral orientations of the boy. This is one of the several core socio-psychological problems underlying this particular program of investigation. Sociological pioneers (e.g., Shaw, McKay, and Sutherland) have focused on the dimensions of social structure and social situations that correlate with high and low delinquency rates, other sociologists (e.g., Reckless and Cohen) have opened exploration of the impact of these situations on the psychological orientations of boys. Psychologist pioneers (e.g., Aichhorn, Healy and Bronner, Redl and Wineman) have explored the internal processes of the deviant youths and have widened their explorations toward the interpersonal situation of the boy and his parents. In his study, Gold has attempted to add another bit of insight into the connection between these often rather disparate concepts and foci of investigation. An effective strategy of social therapy must eventually be based on a comprehensive theory of the processes of connection and interplay between the "sociological factors" and the "psychological factors" in the life situation of the delinquent boy, or group of boys.

Other studies in the series focus on the Negro boy, the delinquent girl, the undetected delinquent, the peer group, the professional youth worker, and on pilot action experiments aimed at the improvement of social practice.

　　　　　　　　　Ronald Lippitt, Research Center for Group Dynamics
　　　　　　　　　Stephen Withey, Survey Research Center

　　　　　　　　　Co-directors of the Inter-center Program on
　　　　　　　　　　Children, Youth, and Family Life

TABLE OF CONTENTS

LIST OF TABLES

TABLE   Page

x

LIST OF FIGURES

Chapter I

THEMES OF AN ESSAY ON JUVENILE DELINQUENCY

This research effort focusses on two questions:

1) Why is it that the sons of lower class families are dispro-portionately responsible for delinquency among American youth? and

2) Can the conditions which give rise to delinquency among lower class boys also be found among higher class delinquents, or do the conditions associated with delinquency in these two sets of boys differ?

It should be clear at the outset that this study was not intended to discover all the causes of delinquency. Rather, it was assumed that any one youngster is delinquent for a complexity of reasons and that the complex of reasons differs from one delinquent to the next. If one considers the variety of behaviors which are called "delin-quent," it seems inconceivable that all instances will some day be found to spring from one single factor or even one small set of fac-tors. For example, here is "delinquency," in just some of its vari-ety, as it was reported in the Flint, Michigan, *Journal*, during the seven months of our field work in Flint.

A 15-year old, teased once too often by his 11-year-old brother about having done time in a state industrial school for boys, fetched his father's rifle and put a bullet through his little brother's head. A 12-year old, described later as "a tough little monkey," and his 10-year-old brother broke into a gun shop and stole two .22-caliber pistols; then four hours later, they used these guns to shoot up an open-air market miles away, killing its owner and wounding two passers-by. Two 16-year olds were picked up for hitchhiking an hour after curfew; the police, noticing bulges under the boys' jackets, discovered the stolen carry-packs of beer which prevented the boys from running fast enough to escape. Two boys, 10 and 8, dashed in and out among cars in a drive-in movie, dropping ignited sparklers at random through open rear windows, leaving a trail of small up-holstery fires and frightened, angry couples. Two boys, both 14, one

1

night led a 12-year old to Swartz Creek and there forced him at knifepoint to lie fully clothed in the cold water. A girl of 16, blond, her ponytail tied with flowers, held up a grocery store with a .32-caliber pistol she did not know how to shoot, but nevertheless carried eighty dollars two blocks away before a policeman, running quietly, caught up with her. A church-school teacher found five teenagers going through his pupils' jackets where they lay beside a ball field, whereupon the youths beat him about the head with softball bats, disfiguring his face and damaging his brain. Three boys, 15, were apprehended as they abondoned a car they had stolen and driven about town until it ran out of gas. Four teenagers, two boys and two girls, were discovered breaking into a gasoline station and under questioning admitted to nineteen burglaries over the previous two months. A boy, 16, and a girl, 15, were found nude one night among bushes in a city park, and the girl's father insisted on a charge of statutory rape because, he said, "that boy is no good."

Thesis

The variety and complexity of juvenile delinquency, along with a desire to engage in empirical research, required that the research problem be limited in scope. So its focus became that set of conditions which might be related to delinquency on the one hand and the social structure of American society on the other. This study is not concerned then with the whole range of personality factors, family factors, and the like which might potentially generate delinquency. Some of these variables got included only because they had the potential of linking social structural variables to delinquent behavior. Indeed, it should be admitted right here that this study was undertaken just in order to discover factors which link social structure to individual behavior, and that the interest in delinquency itself was incidental all along.

The idea that a youngster's position in the social structure of his society helps shape his behavior suggests in turn that social structure has effects on personality development. In fact, there are reasons to believe that differences in personality do exist when people are compared across social strata. While some lower strata individuals are similar in personality to some higher strata individuals, on the average, those in the one strata are different from those in another. One set of evidence comes from a study of the distribution of different types of mental illness in Chicago, in which R. E. L. Faris (1944) found that certain diagnoses more often appeared among the population in the central portions of the city. Inhabitants of the inner city, overwhelmingly in the lower social strata, seem to be more prone to catatonic psychosis than people living elsewhere. A. B. Hollingshead and F. C. Redlich (1958), working in New Haven, found that the higher the social class of treated mental patients, the higher the rates of neuroses, while higher rates of psychoses were found among lower class patients.   D. R. Miller and G. E. Swanson (1958) found that lower class Detroit boys more often expressed aggressive impulses directly, while middle-class boys tended to block aggressive expression.

So while this study took delinquency as its immediate concern, its long-range goal was to contribute to a further understanding of the relationships between personality development and an individual's place in his society.   In the long-range view, delinquency was considered a behavior pattern which perhaps revealed a particular enduring orientation toward the environment, that is, a personality pattern.   An understanding of the part which social structure played in generating a delinquent behavior pattern would, it was hoped, throw some light on the whole social structure-personality process.

It was this long-range goal which largely determined that *patterned delinquent behavior* be studied, rather than isolated delinquent acts.   So, this is a study of repeated delinquents.   The long-range goal also laid down a strategy of research which explored linking processes beginning with a social structural variable, specifically *social status*, and ending with psychological variables, specifically attitudes which seemed relevant to delinquency.   Therefore this is a *social-psychological* study.

Delinquency seemed like an appropriate instance of patterned behavior through which to approach social structure-personality relationships.   First of all, a good deal of thinking about the causes of delinquency has been reported in social science literature, some of it directly concerning its links to social structure.   These theoretical works represented a fund of ideas from which to draw.   Furthermore, many data have been gathered about delinquents, which directly stimulated theory-building and which also could be used to check the results of this study.   One set of data was especially important, namely, that which showed a relationship between social status and the incidence of delinquency.   The data indicated that lower status youngsters are in fact more likely to become delinquent than higher status youngsters.   Here was a behavior pattern which seemed intimately related to a social structural variable, and it was then legitimate to ask "Why?"

Before presenting possible answers to this question, before stating a theory which links social status to delinquency, it is necessary to defend the validity of the fact.   Because not all researchers into juvenile delinquency agree that lower status youngsters are more likely to become delinquent, the remainder of this chapter is an attempt to substantiate the relationship once again.

Social Status and Juvenile Delinquency—
Pro and Con

The fact of lower status over-representation among juvenile delinquents was first strongly indicated by the findings of Shaw and McKay (1929). They discovered that the proportion of boys brought to court for crimes remained constantly higher in Chicago neighborhoods populated by lower status families, even while people themselves moved upward in the social scale and outward from Chicago's Loop. Higher delinquency rates did not move with the population but were properties of lower status neighborhoods irrespective of the individuals or the ethnic groups which lived there. Later work by Shaw and McKay and their associates (1942) uncovered the identical phenomenon in Seattle, Philadelphia, Denver, and elsewhere. Other researchers have found substantially the same association between high juvenile delinquency rates and lower social status (Burgess, 1952; Kvaraceus, 1944; Carr, 1950).

Most objections to the assertion that lower status youngsters are more likely to become delinquent are based on the way delinquency is measured. In all the studies cited above, delinquency rates were figured from the volume of cases handled by police courts, juvenile officers, and social agencies. Skeptics claim that these figures do not accurately reflect the incidence of delinquent acts among social classes. They say that lower status youngsters are more likely to be picked up by police and referred to courts and social agencies, so they show up more often in delinquency statistics; but the data, they say, do not show that these boys more often commit delinquent acts. According to this view, other methods of gathering delinquency data would reveal equal proportions of higher status and lower status delinquents.

Nye, Short, and Olson (1958) conducted a study which they reported to demonstrate this fact. They presented a list of "rules and regulations" to boys and girls attending high schools in one western and one midwestern state and asked them anonymously to "check those that you have broken since beginning grade school." Their interpretation of the data gathered by this method of self-report is that commission of delinquent acts occurs equally often among youth in lower, middle, and upper social strata.

But some reservations might be stated about their conclusions. First, an assumption is necessary that self-report is a more accurate index of the incidence of delinquent acts than official records. But it might be expected that items such as "purposely damaged or destroyed public or private property" would have different meaning for youngsters in different social strata; lower class boys and girls might minimize, even forget, acts of property damage which would be reported by their middle class peers for whom the sanctity of property may be a more salient attitude. Furthermore, the findings of Nye, Short, and Olson may not be directly relevant as a contradiction of findings based on official records, because many instances of delinquent behavior on their check lists would not be considered delinquent by officials. The list of twenty-three rules and regulations includes nine items which only in their extremes would warrant official attention, especially if they were committed by youngsters in grade school: "ever disobeyed your parents"; "had a fist fight with another person"; "ever told a lie"; " 'run away' from home"; "defied your parents' authority (to their face)"; "taken little things (worth less than $2) that did not belong to you"; "taken part in 'gang fights' "; and "hurt or inflicted pain on someone else just to see him squirm." In addition, the checklist includes an item which in neither state involved is a violation of rules and regulations for grade school children: "gone hunting and fishing without a license (or violated other game laws)." So there are ten behavior items in all, out of twenty-three, which official records would not usually include.

On the other hand, two delinquent acts on the list which would, if apprehended, appear in official records—"taken a car for a ride without the owner's knowledge" and "had sex relations with a person of the opposite sex"—were indeed more often reported by lower class boys. Lower class boys also more often admitted they had "skipped school without a legitimate excuse" which might or might not initiate official action, depending on circumstances like a boy's previous record.

Moreover, official records do not testify, nor were they anywhere claimed to testify, to the fact to which Nye, Short, and Olson pay major attention: that significantly more lower status youngsters commit *any one particular kind* of delinquent act. Rather, official records are supposed to demonstrate that these youngsters tend to commit more *of the totality* of those kinds of acts which merit official action. In one analysis of their data, the authors approach this latter issue. They compare over-all scores for a set of seven of the acts among the twenty-three on the checklist and conclude that there is no relationship between these scores and socio-economic status.

But the one table of the seven-item analysis which is presented as typical of the ten tables involved suggests that some relationship between this self-report measure of delinquency and socio-economic level does in fact exist. A re-computation of the data in the published table, presented here in Table 1, reveals that lower status boys more often report committing more of the seven delinquent acts on the list. (The reader may wish to compare Table 1 to the original table [Nye, Table 3:1], noting the difference in the total figures upon which the proportions are based.) Only one cell entry reverses this trend to any extent, the one which shows that one-third of the highest status boys are in the most delinquent category. While this one-third is a little smaller than the proportion of lower status boys in the most delinquent category, it is larger than the proportions of the two

Table 1

Data based on self-report of delinquent behavior suggest that proportionally more lower status boys commit delinquent acts than higher status boys (for boys 12-15, attending state of Washington high schools).[a]

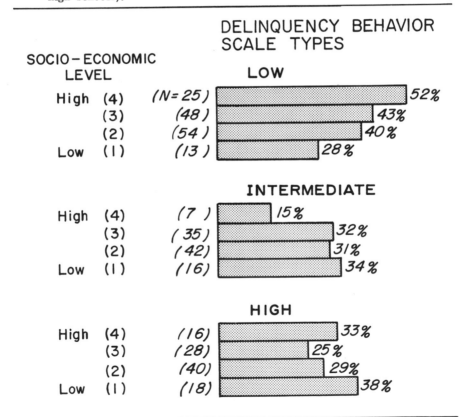

a. Data from Nye (1958), Table 3:1, p. 25. For details of scale construction and index of socio-economic level, see the original source.

middle status categories. A possible explanation for this reversal concerns the delinquent acts involved: in order to get into the most delinquent category, boys must admit either to drinking or to drinking and heterosexual relationships, two kinds of delinquent behaviors perhaps concentrated among boys at the highest and lowest socio-economic levels. Otherwise, the data show that boys in higher socio-economic levels piled up in lower delinquency categories, and lower status boys in higher categories. The authors also allude to at least one other table which demonstrates this trend to an even greater extent.

Furthermore, there is reason to believe that the socio-economic status differences demonstrated by Table 1 may be minimized by the measuring technique, since the seven-item list includes two which, it has been suggested, do not constitute delinquency of an official nature, namely, "defied your parents' authority . . ." and "taken little things (worth less than $2) . . ."

In general, then, the findings of Nye, Short, and Olson do not seem to support the contention that data other than official delinquency figures would reveal no social status differences. The relationship of social status to delinquency seems to be demonstrated by self-report measurement techniques as well.

Still, the argument for social status bias in official delinquency data is a compelling one. Many people share the suspicion that a lower class boy is more likely to have to answer to a judge for the same crime a middle or upper class boy has only to try to explain to a policeman and his parents. An interviewer asked one of the mothers in this study's sample, "When a boy is picked up by the police for doing something wrong, do you think it's handled in the right way in Flint?" and she responded, "They shouldn't always give the rich boys the breaks. They take them home. My boy goes to Detention." The fact that the self-report method of gathering delinquency data does not contradict findings based on official figures is not itself evidence for the adequacy of official figures and should not discourage further probing into the matter. This is especially true since it will be shown now that data gathered in the present research substantiates the assertion that social status bias does indeed exist in the official figures.

Social Status and Delinquency—
another Empirical Test

A brief statement of the way these data were gathered and how they are relevant to the issue is necessary before presenting the data

Table 2

Juvenile male police contact rates of Flint elementary school districts (1957) are inversely related to socio-economic indices (1950 Housing Census) of these school districts; proportion of police contacts (1955-57) who are booked is also inversely related to these socio-economic indices.

Elementary School District[a]	Socio-economic Rank[b]	Police Contacts		Bookings	
		Rate per 1,000	Rank	Pct. Con-tacts	Rank
Pierce	1	12	31	25	31
Longfellow	2	62	24.5	26	30
Civic Park	3	37	30	29	29
Cook	4	81	19	39	21.5
Freeman	5	68	23	54	5.5
Washington	6	58	26	39	21.5
Coolidge	7	49	29	30	28
Garfield	8	62	24.5	48	11.5
Zimmerman	9	57	28	50	9
Durant	10	124	7	35	25
Pierson	11	56	27	33	26.5
McKinley	12	76	20	54	5.5
Cody	13	72	22	36	24
Lewis	14	117	9	58	3.5
Dewey	15	120	8	41	20
Potter	16	83	18	33	26.5
Lincoln	17	84	17	43	18
Stevenson	18	157	3.5	43	18
Homedale	19	75	21	49	10
Martin	20	104	12	45	15.5
Stewart	21	116	10	58	3.5
Dort	22	157	3.5	52	7
Fairview	23	92	14.5	48	11.5
Roosevelt	24	112	11	46	13.5
Walker	25	166	2	37	23
Jefferson	26	92	14.5	46	13.5
Oak	27	135	5	45	15.5
Parkland	28	125	6	62	2
Clark	29	85	16	43	18
Doyle	30	215	1	51	8
Hazelton	31	98	13	66	1
Average		87		44	

a. Four school districts were omitted because city expansion significantly changed their economic statuses since the 1950 Census.

b. Weighted values (average value of dwelling units X per cent owners in the district) are the figures ranked.

Rank-order correlations (τ) of socio-economic indices with delinquency contact rates of elementary school districts:

Socio-economic Index (from Housing Census, 1950)	τ	p level
Average value of dwelling units....	-.30	.008
Per cent owners	-.48	.0007
Weighted value	-.56	.0003

themselves. The data were obtained through the cooperation of the Flint Juvenile Bureau, which handles all instances of law violation involving youth under seventeen in the city of Flint. This includes both crimes committed by these youths and some types of crimes perpetrated on them, such as neglect; only crimes allegedly committed by youth were included in the analysis to follow, and each boy is included only once, even if he was charged with several crimes. When a youth is contacted on suspicion of committing a crime, whether he is contacted on the street, in school, at home, brought to the Bureau, or wherever, the "contact" is written up on "the blotter." Not all of these "contacts" result in arrests, but those that do are converted into "bookings." Furthermore, not all "bookings" become Probate Court cases; many never appear before the judge. But appearance in court presupposes a "booking." And, of course, of those boys who appear in court, few are institutionalized. The criteria upon which "contacts" become "bookings"; "bookings," "court cases"; and "court cases," "institutionalized delinquents" will be discussed later.

The point is that each decision for conversion shunts a boy through to the next step in the process. The data indicate that whether a boy is shunted through to the next step, at least at one point in the process, depends in part on his social class origin.

A comparison of the first column with the last column in Table 2 demonstrates this point. The first column contains the socio-economic ranks of Flint elementary school districts, based on the values of dwelling units and the proportion of home-owners in the district as determined by the housing census made in 1950; Pierce, ranked 1, is the highest ranked on socio-economic status, which indicates that people of higher social status make up the greatest share of residents there. The last column contains the contacts-to-bookings ranks for these same elementary school districts, based on the proportion of contacts with boys living in that district which are converted to bookings: Pierce, ranked 31, has the lowest proportion, the 25 per cent in the fourth column; the lowest social status district, Hazelton, with more than twice that proportion, ranks highest. Comparison of the ranks on socio-economic status with the ranks on proportion of bookings reveals a strong tendency for boys living in higher status school districts to be booked less often. When Kendall's statistic for rank-order comparisons, tau, was applied to these data (Siegel, 1956), it indicated that this covariation of the two rank orders could have occurred merely by chance only once out of a hundred times. That is, it is unlikely that this is a chance relationship and so some substantive factor is probably responsible for it.

It has been suggested that the factor which accounts for this finding is that police and court procedures disadvantage the lower status boy. But at least one other factor could be determining it: Lower status boys might be committing more "serious" crimes, which are more likely to demand official action. Unfortunately, it was impossible to study "seriousness" for we and the police were unable to determine the seriousness of a crime with any surety, feeling that many complex factors, of which the act itself is only one, must be considered in each case to determine its seriousness. These multiple considerations might themselves indicate that the seriousness of the crime is not the important factor which converts contacts to bookings.

Table 3 casts further doubt on the seriousness hypothesis by showing that about the same proportion of higher status and lower status boys were apprehended for various types of crimes. The distribution of youthful crimes in the five lowest socio-economic districts was compared to the distribution in the five highest ranked. But since three of the five lowest status were also predominantly Negro, the five lowest status white school districts and the five low status Negro districts were separately compared to the five highest status white districts. The average proportions over each set of five districts for each crime category are presented.

There are some differences in the distributions of types of crimes. "Property destruction" is the most frequent crime committed by boys from higher status districts, while "assault and armed robbery" are the modal crimes for boys from lower status Negro districts. But boys from lower status neighborhoods also tend to run away more often, which is not an offense usually booked. In general, because differences are small, it is doubtful that they account for all of the strong relationship between booking rates and socio-economic status.

Table 3

Juvenile delinquents living in the five highest status, predominantly white school districts are apprehended for a somewhat different
pattern of crimes than those from the five lowest status districts;
juveniles from the five low status, predominantly Negro districts
show still another slightly different pattern.

Offense	Per Cent in Five Highest White Districts (N = 426)	Per Cent in Five Lowest White Districts (N = 1040)	Per Cent in Five Low Negro Districts (N = 680)
Break and enter	11	9	8
Auto theft.............	4	4	3
Shoplift	3	4	6
Larceny, unarmed robbery .	15	14	14
Property destruction	20	12	13
Arson	1	1	—
Assault; personal injury; armed robbery........	8	6	14
Threat to injure; molesting .	1	1	1
Sex offenses	3	5	3
Truancy.............	1	2	3
Incorrigible; family trouble.	4	4	5
Runaway..............	5	9	10
Gang activity or fight.....	1	1	1
Trespass	1	1	1
Disturbance	7	4	4
Escape from custody	1	1	1
Parole violation	3	2	3
Carry concealed weapons ..	1	1	1
Unspecified delinquency ...	10	12	7
Drinking..............	1	1	1
	100	100	100

While this evidence weakens the seriousness hypothesis, it is
not conclusive. While there are no great differences among categories of crimes committed by boys from different social strata, differences in seriousness may lurk still within categories. That is,
lower status and higher status boys may commit about the same
proportion of assaults, but the former may make more vicious attacks than the latter and so provoke sterner penalties. The seriousness hypothesis is still tenable, but nevertheless another explanation may prove more valid: *differential booking rates among social
strata depend on differential judgments of the effectiveness of family
controls among social strata.*

This hypothesis rests on the assumption that the usual police procedure allows a youngster's family to keep him from misbehaving again whenever it seems his family will be effective. To depend on judges, probation officers, and custodians of juvenile institutions is generally considered by all odds the poorer alternative. But the phrase "generally considered" covers the crucial issue; for the authorities continually must make judgments about the potential effectiveness of families for controlling their children. Where the judgment is negative, the youngster is moved on through official channels. The total percentage figure of contacts which are booked, the fourth column of Table 2, indicates that a negative judgment was made, at this stage in the procedure, in 44 per cent of the cases.

The nature of the criteria for determining whether or not a family can provide effective control, whether it is a "good risk," may create the social class bias in the figures. Probably one of the most important criteria is past performance: if a boy is a repeater, he is more likely to be booked, not so much because recidivism indicates that he is an inveterate delinquent, but perhaps because it demonstrates the unreliability of family control in his case. The fact seems to be that lower status boys are more likely to be repeaters and for this reason more likely to be booked; whether this actually indicates that lower status families are less effective instruments of control will be discussed in some detail in Chapter VI.

Another criterion of "good risk" among families may be their "intactness," that is, whether both parents are present. Since lower status families are less often intact, they are less often regarded as "good risks." Similar estimations operate for criteria such as a history of criminality in the family, among parents or sibs; drunkenness of parents; extent of supervision over the boy, which is judged less if both parents work full time; financial ability to make whatever special arrangements seem necessary for treatment, which might range from psychotherapy to incarceration in a military academy; and so on. All of these are less likely to result in a judgment of "good risk" for a lower status family than for a higher status family. Hence, lower status boys would more often be "booked" and shunted on for further official action.

Does this demonstration of a social class bias in police procedure support the critics of court records used as delinquency rate data? Clearly, it does. But it does not necessarily mean that this bias accounts *completely* for the greater proportion of lower status boys among official delinquents. Perhaps some of this lower class over-representation in juvenile court records is still an accurate reflection of the relative incidence of delinquent behavior. Some of the data already presented indirectly suggest that, even when the bias in the records is minimized, lower class boys will still appear among delinquents more often. These are the data on "contacts."

Kobrin (1951), an associate of Chicago's Institute for Juvenile Research, asserts that police complaint records are probably the most inclusive measure of delinquency obtainable, although they surely are not complete. "Contact" figures from the Flint Juvenile Bureau correspond to what Kobrin means by "complaint records." Delinquency rates based on these "contact" figures demonstrate that boys living in lower status elementary school districts are more likely to be contacted than boys living in higher status districts. The third column of Table 2 contains the districts' ranks for the "contact rates," which are themselves in the second column. Kendall's rank-order statistic indicates that the correspondence of the contact rank order with socio-economic rank order could have occurred by chance three times in a thousand.

Undoubtedly possible sources of bias in contact figures can be suggested. But the fact remains that in every type of delinquency rate examined so far—based on institutionalized delinquents, court cases, arrests, contacts, or self-report—lower status boys are over-represented. At this point it seems justifiable to accept the fact, at least for now. It should be clear that this fact served as the basis of the research reported here. Its acceptance is prompted even further by isolation in this study of some reasons *why* more lower status boys commit crimes.

Overview of the Study

An extensive review of the literature on delinquency suggested that the factors associated with delinquency might usefully be categorized as *control* factors or *provocation* factors: that is, as forces which keep a boy from becoming delinquent and forces which encourage him to become delinquent. A few control and a few provocation factors were selected for study here by the criteria that these factors might be associated both with social status on the one hand and delinquency on the other.

Attraction, a positive attitude of boy toward a source of influence, is assumed to be the foundation of effective control. In this study, attraction to the community and to the family were explored in their relationship to social status and delinquency. It was found that community resources with perhaps the most relevance to youth, in the areas of education and recreation, are so distributed that lower status boys could find the community less attractive to them and hence, less effectively controlling. But it also appears that, while educational and recreational facilities are differentially distributed by social class, this has no clear effect on boys' attraction to their community. Finally, it is argued that the community as such is not a crucial source of delinquency control and that the distribution of its recreational and educational facilities do not shape the distribution of delinquency to any appreciable degree.

Attraction to the family, on the other hand, seems to be a crucial variable in determining a boy's vulnerability to delinquency. Attraction to his family helps to determine the degree to which a boy is influenced by or controlled by his family. Furthermore, attraction to the family seems to depend to some extent on the social status of the family, lower status families having lower attraction potential. The very nature of the father's job by which a family is assigned its social status, the power structure within the family, and the discipline techniques employed by the parents appear to be specific family variables which link social status to son's attraction to family.

Recent trends in the delinquency literature led to special consideration of occupational opportunities as a factor which might provoke delinquency. The findings suggest that delinquent boys more than non-delinquent boys are subject to feelings of personal failure, prompted by their estimates of how successful they will be by common social standards of occupational success. Furthermore, the experiences which suggest to boys that they are and will be failures occur more often in the lives of lower status rather than higher status boys. These experiences have mainly to do with achievement in school. It is suggested finally that delinquent behavior is especially suited to relieve a boy of the psychological burden of feelings of personal failure.

Since lower social status seems to be related to lower family attraction and more feelings of personal failure, it follows that lower status boys will more often be delinquent, the fact this study set out to explain. It further appears that these same factors of lower family attraction and feelings of personal failure appear among higher status delinquents, too. However, since they seem to appear less frequently among higher status boys generally, it follows that fewer of them will become delinquent.

The rest of this report elaborates upon and qualifies the foregoing brief summary of findings. Chapter II presents the salient features of the literature review which yielded promising clues to which variables should be studied.   Chapters III and IV describe the research methods.   Chapter V discusses recreational and educational resources in the community, their distribution, and their relationship to delinquency.   Chapter VI takes up the family as an agency of delinquency control.   Chapter VII presents material on boys' estimates of their occupational futures and their relationship to delinquency. In Chapter VIII, some issues concerning which-is-causing-what, raised in earlier chapters, are discussed.   Chapter IX includes a detailed summary of the findings based on some familiarity with the terminology and the data of the study; and some suggestions about what needs to be done next.

Chapter II

A SOCIAL-PSYCHOLOGICAL APPROACH
TO JUVENILE DELINQUENCY

The purpose of this chapter is to re-create the context of ideas in which this research proceeded. Only some of this context pertained specifically to juvenile delinquency. It included ideas about deviancy in general, and more generally still, about how social-psychology might illuminate problems like deviancy and delinquency.

An understanding of the context in which the research work takes place is necessary in order to understand the research itself. Such contexts, whether they include rigorous theory or not, surround any research. After all, the researcher who wishes to learn the causes of juvenile delinquency might pursue an infinite range of possibilities: economic cycles, birth trauma, war and peace, birth order, neuroticism among mothers, racial composition of neighborhoods, the nature of boys' companions, or the shape of boys' bodies, to name a few which have in fact been researched in relation to delinquency. But any one research project can include only a limited number of variables to study. The researcher's selection of variables upon which to focus is largely determined by the context of ideas in which he works. The intent of the chapter is to make explicit the salient elements of the context which guided this research.

A Field-Theory Model of Delinquent Behavior

An important aspect of the orientation of this research is its field-theory approach to understanding behavior. The individual is portrayed as behaving in a dynamic field of forces, and his behavior is conceptualized as movement toward or away from his goals (Lewin, 1951). Forces representing either motivations of the individual or environmental pressures drive and restrain the individual's movement in certain directions.

Figure 1 is a simple illustration of a field-theory model of a situation. Suppose a person, P, is hungry. At the moment, he knows he is "hungry," here diagrammed as being in region I, but that he might be "not hungry," in region IV. The unpleasantness of hunger, force F_1, is a driving force tending to move P from region

I to region IV. Now, P might go to a restaurant to eat or put a coin in a nearby candy machine; that is, he may get to region IV by going through region II or III. Unfortunately, P is down to his last dime, so there is a strong reason for not going to the restaurant, which is represented by restraining force F_2. So P will probably take the path I-III-IV.

In its most general form, the field-theoretical approach is a formulation of problems about the directionality of *any behavior*. It

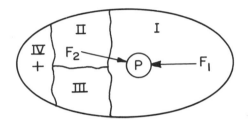

Fig. 1.   An illustrative diagram of a field-theory approach.

may be used to schematize diverse situations like a boy raiding the cooky jar and a young man studying to become a doctor, a dog detouring around a wire fence to get at a bone and a woman deciding what types of meat to serve her family. It becomes a schematization of *deviant behavior* only when certain of the restraining forces are specified. When an individual moves against restraining forces which originate in disapproval shared by a group of others, the individual's behavior is deviant with reference to that group.

Deviant behavior can be schematized in two ways, depending on whether the individual's goals or the means by which he arrives at his goals are disapproved. Figures 2a and 2b illustrate this point. In Figure 2a, individual P is driven by forces F_1 and F_2 toward goal regions I and II. Region I stands for a goal approved by

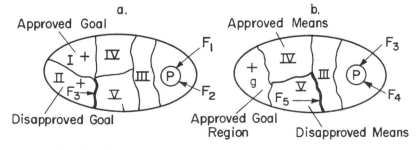

Fig. 2.   Field-theory diagrams of two types of deviancy.

a relevant group, and region II, for a disapproved goal. At the boundary of region II is set up a barrier consisting of the force F_3, the disapproval of the relevant group. In Figure 2b, the goal region may be generally approved, but individual P has alternative paths to reaching his goal, path III-IV-g or path III-V-g. The means represented by Region IV are generally approved, but the means represented by Region V are disapproved and a barrier consisting of disapproval force F_5 is set up at its boundary. In either case, however, movement through the barriers representing social disapproval is deviant behavior.

The schematization becomes a model of *delinquent behavior* when disapproved forces and the individual P are further specified. Delinquent behavior is movement through a barrier which represents social disapproval codified into formal rules, or law, and when the individual is defined by the law as a nonadult. That is, when someone who is regarded by the law as a juvenile or youth breaks the law, this is juvenile delinquent behavior.

Reference to Figure 2b will help sum up this discussion so far. Forces F_3, F_4, and F_5 are acting upon the individual P to move him in one direction or another. These forces, acting upon a boy, might be the urging of his friends, an inner feeling of anger, or a desire to drive a car; or they might be a fear of being put in jail, or a concern about not getting into college if he gets a police record. Some of these forces are pushing the boy toward stealing a car; the others are restraining him from it.

This model might apply to any potentially deviant behavior. One set of forces, called *provocations,* drives the individual toward violating some standard of proper behavior; another set, called *controls,* restrains him. But it can be seen that the specific kinds of provocations and controls which act as forces in a particular situation change, depending on the individual and the standard involved. The forces relevant to provoke a boy to behave in a certain way may not so provoke an adult, nor would all the forces which constrain boys to obey rules at home be appropriate in school. In all cases, however, it is clear that when the strength of provoking forces exceeds the strength of controlling forces, the individual will deviate.

Theoretically, the strength of provocations and the strength of controls are independent from one another. One may find boys for whom provocations to become delinquent are quite strong but high levels of controls prevent them from becoming delinquent, or boys for whom provocations are strong and controls weak so that they do become delinquent, and so on. Provocations and controls are not necessarily correlated. Where conditions are such that strong provocations are *coincidental* with weak controls, boys are most likely to become delinquent.

This field-theoretical formulation sets two important conditions for a study of delinquency. First, it may incorporate a multi-causal theory of delinquency. While it would not be a violation of the model to posit a single driving force toward delinquency, it is consistent also to suppose that many different forces may provoke delinquent behavior and many different forces may be invoked to restrain it. The multi-causal supposition is favored here. An assumption underlying this research is that various patterns of provocative and controlling forces may result in delinquent behavior. These patterns need have only one thing in common: the strength of the provocations exceed the strength of controls (see Carr, 1950, p. 160, for another statement of this formulation). Not all researchers into delinquency accept a multi-causal assumption, as a review of some of the literature will show shortly.

The second implication of the field-theoretical approach is that provocations and controls must be operating in the psychological field of a youngster *in the present* in order to be effective in generating or restraining delinquent behavior. On the one hand, this makes unacceptable a driving force which represents, for example, maternal neglect during infancy; for previous neglect is not a contemporaneous force in the psychological field of an adolescent boy. This is not to say that such neglect is an unimportant factor but rather to insist that present residues of previous neglect—chronic hostility, anxiety, or whatever—be specified and demonstrated.

The second implication of field-theory has been perhaps even more important than the first in the determination of the strategy of this research. The field-theoretical stipulation of psychological contemporaneousness requires that variables be translated into psychological terms before they may be represented as forces in the psychological field. Directly pertinent to this implication is the problem of the appropriate representation of the *social status* condition of a boy as it affects his behavior. Here is the focal problem of this research. To ask why relatively more lower status than higher status boys become delinquent is to ask what kinds of provocative and controlling forces are set up in boys' psychological fields by the condition of lower or higher status which is a collective, not a psychological condition. The question requires for an answer explication of the processes by which a social structural variable, social status, ceases to be only a potential force or *boundary condition* and becomes a set of psychological forces. Making such translations is the assignment of social-psychology.

A Social-psychological Orientation

Social-psychology, as it is thought of here, is the study of the individual in his social environment. This definition may be clarified by Figure 3. The core of the figure, the core and central concern of social-psychology, is the individual. This is the heart of the "psychology" in "social-psychology." The individual is depicted as psychologists depict him, as having needs, motives, sensations, perceptions, capacities, and so forth. But to the social-psychologist, *skills,* the individual's developed capacities to manipulate his

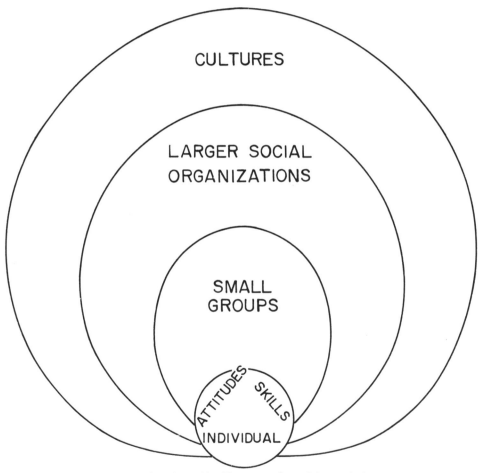

Fig. 3. A schematic diagram of social-psychology.

environment, and *attitudes*, his feelings about the objects in his environment, are the focal intra-individual or psychological concepts. It is possible to think about the effects of the environment on the individual as changes in his attitudes or skills. Similarly it is possible to capture the effects of intra-individual variables like motives and percepts in their effects on attitudes and skills.

The social environment, which is the other part of the relationship which interests the social-psychologist, is an environment peopled in two ways: it is an environment of people, and of objects which have people-meaning. The people-meaning aspect of objects can be illustrated in this way: when a boy jumps the ignition lock of a stranger's car and drives the car away, he is not stealing a complex of metals, chemicals, fabrics, and glass; he is stealing something with which he can impress his friends and impress himself and is valuable to him only for its social meaning.

The individual participates in three different levels of his social environment, as Figure 3 denotes. He is a member of small, face-to-face groups, such as his friends, his club, and his family. He fits into wider social organizations, all of whose members he does not know personally: the corporation in which he works, his community, his nation-state. And he participates in a culture like Western culture and subcultures like American, carrying much of their current ideology and taking advantage of their current stage of technological development. It is useful to distinguish these three levels of social environment because the individual's participation in each level is different, and they work upon him in different ways.

Figure 3 suggests that the individual has by far the most frequent and most important contacts with his social environment as a member of small, face-to-face groups. Most of his shaping by the social environment is accomplished by the intimate groups to which he belongs. Wider social structures have some direct effects by such means as providing him with certain facilities to utilize, as a community provides a boy with a school, or a man with a job. Cultures have their major direct effects by the broadcast of ideas through the mass media of newspapers, radio, television, and the motion pictures; for not only events, jokes, and stories are transmitted, but also a limited range of living-style alternatives, political ideas, and social values. Still, research up to now indicates that social structures and cultures are effective mainly in the way they shape experiences in the small groups to which the individual belongs.

The approach to juvenile delinquency taken here regarded boys' behaviors as products of their participation in the small groups, social structures, and cultures which are theirs. More specifically, attention was primarily paid to their social status, their place in some related social structures, how this is affected by the cultural ideology about them, and how it affects the groups to which they belong. These were considered the boundary conditions relevant to boys' behaviors. The aim of this research was to isolate some aspects of these boundary conditions specifically relevant to delinquent behavior and to trace the processes by which these become imbedded in boys' attitudes and there provoke or control delinquent behavior. Presentation of the particular social-psychological processes which were studied here depends first on the definition of two key elements in these processes, *social status* and *juvenile delinquency,* and on a review of the literature which guided the selection of process-links to be researched.

The Meaning of "Social Status"

A boy's social status was determined in this study by his father's occupation. But the implications of status measured in this way go beyond simply the kind of job his father holds. A boy's status places him among an interrelated set of probabilities which he shares with other boys of the same status but not with boys of another status. The income his family will receive in the coming year will probably be closer to the income of other families of his social status than of incomes of other families. The level of education his parents had and that he is likely to gain is probably more like other boys in his status position. The kind of job he will take and the status he will achieve on his own is probably more like other boys who spring from families of similar status than like boys who get started from a different position in the social structure. And so on, reaching, as was pointed out in Chapter I, into the probabilities of holding certain attitudes, values, and basic modes of adapting to his environment.

The central dimension of status, as this concept is used here, is prestige. It is in this connection that the adjectives "higher" and "lower" are assigned to status positions. Status, as it is used here, refers to a *boy's prestige position in the social structures of American society and the Flint community, as it is determined by his father's occupation.* It has implications for his current life patterns and for his future life chances. His status probably shapes his own feelings of self-respect. Having been carried this far, the concept of "status" will be left for the moment to consider the meaning of "juvenile delinquency."

The Meaning of "Juvenile Delinquency"

In his recent book with W. C. Kvaraceus, *Delinquent Behavior: Culture and the Individual* (1959), W. B. Miller defined juvenile delinquency as "behavior by nonadults which violates specific legal norms or the norms of a particular societal institution with sufficient frequency and/or seriousness as to provide a firm basis for legal action against the behaving individual or group" (p. 54). This was the definition used in the present study. The selection of this phenomenon for study, instead of isolated delinquent acts, follows from the aim of this research as it was stated in Chapter I, to study *patterned behavior* as a clue to personality patterns.

A juvenile delinquent, then, is not just a youngster who has misbehaved. Nor is he a youngster who has broken just any law. According to this definition, it makes no difference if the boy has been apprehended; he is a juvenile delinquent if he has behaved so that upon his apprehension, authorities would take legal action against him. This implies that police contact data do not include all delinquents, and certainly arrest files, court cases, and institutional roles include progressively fewer of the delinquents in the population.

L. J. Carr, in his book *Delinquency Control* (1950), presented "a target for consistent reference," which has helped keep the meanings of "delinquent" in order. Carr's "target" is reproduced here as Figure 4. According to Miller's definition, some but not all of the "legal delinquents" (circle 3) are "juvenile delinquents." Many of these do not break the law often enough or seriously enough to be called "juvenile delinquents" under Miller's definition. Police contact files include Carr's "detected delinquents" (circle 4); court records include "alleged delinquents" (circle 6); "adjudged delinquents" (circle 7) include institutionalized offenders, as well as youngsters on probation and parole and youngsters whom the court has returned to their homes under no official surveillance. The juvenile delinquents studied in the present work come from Carr's "detected delinquent," "alleged delinquent," and "adjudged delinquent" categories. They were chosen to represent all those boys who fit Miller's definition of "delinquent." These apprehended delinquents represent delinquents in general to the extent that the forces which provoke and control delinquent behavior are similar among boys who are caught and those who are not.

Restatement of the Research Aim

With the presentation of field-theoretical and social-psychological orientations, and definitions given for "status" and "juvenile

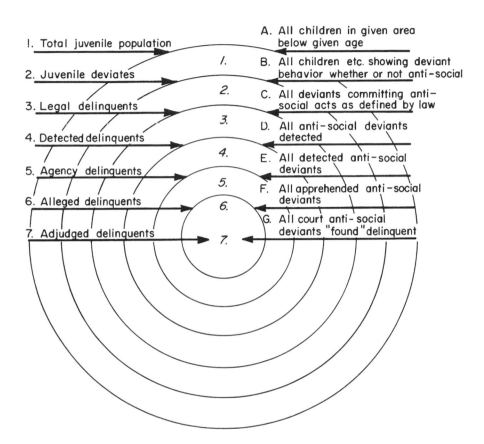

Fig. 4.   Carr's target for consistent reference.[a]

---

a. From L. J. Carr, *Delinquency Control*, p. 90.

delinquency," it is now possible to restate in clearer terms the aims of this research.   Its aims were to isolate some of the attitudes and skills which provoke or control repeated and/or serious violations of the law by boys; to uncover associations between these attitudes and skills and the positions of boys' families in the prestige hierarchy of the occupational structure; to trace some processes by which social status is linked to boys' attitudes and skills through cultural, social-structural, and small-group elements of their social environment; to discover reasons why lower social status more often creates those kinds of provocations and controls associated with delinquency; and to ascertain whether the patterns of provocations and controls associated with juvenile delinquency differ from lower to higher status boys.

How does a social scientist know where to look for the factors causing the phenomenon he wants to explain? Here, specifically, what kinds of provocations and controls are likely to be relevant to juvenile delinquency? Again, the context within which a researcher works helps steer him. Part of this context is the history of research in his field, the reports of other researchers who have proposed explanations and perhaps tested their accuracy. A brief survey of representative thinking and research on juvenile delinquency will suggest several causative factors. It will be helpful in making some order out of the literature to apply both the field-theoretical model of delinquency, sorting suggested causes into categories of driving and restraining forces; and the social-psychological orientation, sorting forces by their sources in the social environment, whether cultural, social structural, or small group.

Some Previous Thought and Research on Delinquency

Published material on juvenile delinquency, by social scientists alone, is voluminous. In his text *Juvenile Delinquency,* Tappan (1949), lists 196 separate titles which clearly refer to the etiology of delinquency, and several times that number more or less relevant to the subject. No attempt will be made here to review all the literature. Rather, a very small number of studies which seem to be central to or representative of approaches to the delinquency problem will be discussed as they are relevant to the focus of the present research. A great deal of this review was developed from material in Bordua's "Delinquency Theory and Research in the U.S.: Major Trends since 1930" (1957).

It has been pointed out that C. R. Shaw and H. D. McKay (*op. cit.*) were the first to demonstrate empirically an association between juvenile delinquency and social status. Their speculations on the causality of delinquency, offered in the course of interpreting their data, seem to fit easily into a model of provocations and controls. Boys are provoked to delinquency, they wrote, in part by a desire for social status. Boys living in lower status neighborhoods are more likely to feel deprived of status, so are more likely to become delinquent. At the same time, controls are weakened because these boys have little prestige to lose by getting into trouble with the law, but much prestige to gain among their fellows by virtue of their daring behavior, and in wider social circles by virtue of the material goods they might acquire. Social control is even further weakened, they continued, because other members of the groups in which they participate are also lower status and share rather than disapprove of the attitudes which give rise to delinquency. So Shaw and McKay did in theory link their social structural findings about delinquency rates in urban areas to social-psychological principles, but they did not study psychological variables directly.

E. H. Sutherland (1939) proposed what is essentially a theory of social control. He wrote:

> A person becomes delinquent because of an excess of definitions favorable to violation of law over definitions unfavorable to violations of law. . . . When persons become criminal, they do so because of contacts with criminal patterns and also because of isolation from anticriminal patterns. Any person inevitably assimilates the surrounding culture unless other patterns are in conflict [p. 6].

Sutherland called this principle *differential association with criminal elements*. With this principle, Sutherland pressed the point that delinquent skills and delinquent attitudes were learned through intimate contact with people who were already delinquent. Further, he posited differential association as the single cause of delinquency; all other factors associated with boys becoming delinquent operated by putting them in greater contact with delinquent than with non-delinquent others. As far as the principle of differential association is concerned, then, Sutherland pointed to a process-link between the small-group level of the social environment and the individual boy's attitudes and skills.

Sutherland linked social status to delinquency by including it among those factors which tended to increase association with delinquent patterns. He pointed out that lower status youngsters reside in areas of the city where delinquent patterns, manifested by gangs, prostitutes, adult criminals, and such are most dense. Why should these elements congregate in particular areas of a city? In explanation, Sutherland invoked the concept of culture conflict. Lower status areas characteristically contain immigrants and native minorities whose norms are more likely to be in conflict with those of the larger society. The culture conflict concept then explains the concentration of crime in an area; it is the explanation, on a culture level, of delinquency *rates*. Differential association explains the criminal behavior of *a person*.

Sutherland recognized that his views created some problems. One was: "How did crime begin in the first place. . . . It can't be diffused until it originates, and differential association does not explain its origin" (Sutherland, 1942, p. 24). His answer was that delinquent patterns did not begin as such, but began as accepted ways of behaving and were then imported into an alien culture which defined it as delinquent. That is, Sutherland consistently returned to the culture-conflict source of criminality.

Another problem was why many boys do not become delinquent, even in high delinquency areas. Sutherland wrote:

> It is difficult to explain why some of the boys in the [high delinquency rate] neighborhood do not become delinquent. One factor is the limitation on contact with delinquents, even in the most delinquent areas. A delinquent area is practically never solidly delinquent; rather, there are certain streets or parts of streets on which at a particular time the delinquents reside, and on other streets the children may associate with each other in relative isolation from the delinquents. Sometimes one or more national groups within a general residential area are isolated from the rest of the population, or a few members of one such group may be isolated within a larger area of another nationality. Also, some children are kept from frequent or intimate contact with delinquents because of their retiring, quiet, and unaggressive disposition. Others are kept from such associations by careful and capable parents or siblings. Some of the children may refrain from delinquency because they have formed attachments at school with teachers, or at other agencies with other leaders; and their interests have been developed and their lives organized around lawful activities, so that association with delinquents is not attractive to them. Finally, whether contact and association with delinquents develop or contacts and association with lawful agencies is often a matter of sheer chance [Sutherland, 1959, pp. 142-143].

It is clear that Sutherland returned again and again to factors which affect boys' associations with other delinquents to explain why one boy becomes delinquent and another not.

Sutherland's theory everywhere denies the possibility that significant amounts of criminal behavior are inventions. Lower status neighborhoods have high crime rates, because criminal behavior was imported from cultures where it is not criminal; boys become delinquents because of association with established criminal patterns. In terms of the field-theory orientation, Sutherland recognized no provocations to delinquent behavior as such. However, one of his students and colleagues, Albert K. Cohen, expanded the theory in this direction. Cohen's theory will be outlined in some detail now because, more than any one other theory, this one guided the exploration of status-linked provocations in this research.

The problem Cohen set for himself, in his book *Delinquent Boys,* was not to explain why certain boys become delinquent while

others did not, but rather the related problem of why delinquent patterns of behavior become characteristic among boys living in some
areas of a city and not among others. Cohen seems largely to have
agreed with Sutherland that the presence of delinquent gangs in an
area increases the likelihood that other boys will become delinquent.
But Cohen did not suggest that all delinquent behavior is imported
initially as non-delinquent behavior. Rather, he recognized some
forces in the lives of lower status boys which encourage the fresh
formation of delinquent gangs. By positing such forces, Cohen im-
plicitly presented reasons for individual boys being provoked to delinquency, although explicitly he emphasized, along with Sutherland,
that association with other delinquents is a necessary support for
delinquent behavior.

Cohen's theory is built on his description of the delinquent patterns which exist. He has described this pattern of behavior as
"non-utilitarian, malicious, and negativistic," characterized by a
"short-run hedonism." Groups of boys steal things, not for their
material value, but to enhance the status of the thieves; they destroy
property, not to express a specific anger, but rather to flout the
rules of the larger social order, to express disdain for the rules.
Cohen called this pattern of collective behavior *the delinquent subculture*; its hallmark "is the explicit and wholesale repudiation of
middle-class standards and the adoption of their very antithesis"
(Cohen, 1955, p. 129).

Why Cohen chose to focus on the delinquent subculture rather
than on individual delinquents might be understood in the historical
context. As a student and colleague of E. H. Sutherland, he recognized that, in order to make the theory of differential association
account for the fact of greater lower-class participation in delinquency, it would be necessary to show that greater opportunity for association with delinquents existed in lower-class neighborhoods. Cohen suggested that greater opportunity for differential association
exists in working-class neighborhoods because in these neighborhoods conditions are most favorable for the *development* of the delinquent subculture. The location of the delinquent subculture among
working-class boys is the main thesis of Cohen's book *Delinquent
Boys*.

Cohen addressed himself first to the conditions under which
any culture will develop. He asserted that "the crucial condition
for the emergence of new cultural forms is the existence, *in effective interaction with one another, of a number of actors with similar problems of adjustment" (ibid.,* p. 59). According to Cohen, individuals make tentative attempts to solve their problems, but drop

their solutions if they find no support among others. Some solutions are picked up by others, however, and become crystallized as approved patterns of behavior among a group of individuals who share the same problems. Such is the process by which delinquent patterns of behavior become established as a subculture.

What are the problems which working-class boys share and for which they develop a delinquent solution? Cohen has been clear:

> These problems are chiefly status problems: certain children are denied status in the respectable society because they cannot meet the criteria of the respectable status system. The delinquent subculture deals with these problems by providing criteria of status which these children *can* meet [*ibid.*, p. 121].

In what way are working-class children "denied status?" According to Cohen, this occurs largely through inadequate training for the competition for status. He noted that modal child-rearing patterns differ from one social class to another. Working-class families are not so likely to develop the attitudes and skills in their children which will prime them for the achievement of respectability.

> "Planning" and "foresight" on the part of his parents are not so likely to be evident to the working-class as to the middle-class child [*ibid.*, p. 96].

> [The working person] is less likely to possess, to value or to cultivate the polish, the sophistication, the fluency, the "good appearance" and the "personality" so useful in "selling oneself" and manipulating others in the middle-class world [*ibid.*, p. 97].

> One of the situations in which children of all social levels come together and compete for status in terms of the same set of middle-class criteria and in which working-class children are most likely to be found wanting is in the school [*ibid.*, p. 112].

Cohen asserted that, despite their handicaps in the competition for status, most working-class youngsters nevertheless wish to achieve status as it is defined by middle-class criteria.

> Indeed, it seems probable that most children in American society, of whatever class, assimilate to some degree the middle-class value system. Some assimilate it in almost "pure" form, others in various attenuated versions and various uneasy combinations with the working-class value system, sometimes submerged by the working-class system but rarely altogether stifled [*ibid.*, p. 104].

> To the degree to which [a working-class child] values middle-class status, either because he values the good opinion of middle-class persons or because he has to some degree internalized middle-class standards himself, he faces a problem of adjustment and is in the market for a "solution" [*ibid.*, p. 119].

The delinquent subculture, we suggest, is a way of dealing with the problems of adjustment we have described [*ibid.*, p. 121].

Applying the general model of deviant behavior, it seems that Cohen's theory emphasizes provocations, forces which drive boys to violate legal standards.   According to the theory, the major provocation is status deprivation.   One of the strong points of the theory is that it not only explains why boys become deviant but also why they become delinquent.   This is, the theory not only locates the delinquent subculture in lower status neighborhoods, it also explains why it takes the particular form that it does.

Cohen's theory is social-psychological, as that term has been used here.   It demonstrates the relevance of cultural criteria of prestige to the status hierarchy of social organization, and it shows how the status problem which is thus created gives rise to small groups of boys which have certain delinquent goals.   As far as explaining why individuals become delinquent, the theory seems to suggest two possibilities.   It has been pointed out that Cohen explicitly intends his theory to explain the delinquent subculture, not individual delinquency.   Having established the location and form of this subculture, it is possible then to explain individual delinquency by Sutherland's principle of differential association.

If Cohen's theory explains individual delinquency only insofar as shared status problems give rise to a delinquent subculture within which individuals may learn delinquent behavior, then it does not apply to middle-class delinquency; for the status problems which are said to give rise to the delinquent subculture are too rare in middle-class neighborhoods to create a flourishing delinquent subculture. But if the theory predicts that individuals with these status problems will become delinquents, whether or not they get the support to establish or to join an established delinquent subculture, then one would expect that those few middle-class boys with status problems will become delinquent.   When he wrote *Delinquent Boys,* Cohen's opinion was that his theory probably could not be extended to explain middle-class delinquency, but he was not sure.

Cohen theorized that middle-class "delinquency" is not really the same phenomenon as working-class "delinquency" and stems from quite different causes.   He wrote:

It seems to us more likely that subcultural delinquency in the different social classes will prove to be kin but by no means identical twins. We would anticipate that subcultural delinquency in the middle class will turn out to differ in quality as well as frequency from that which we found in the working class; that is, subcultural delinquency in the different social classes is a qualitatively different response to qualitatively different problems arising in different contexts of communication and interaction [*ibid.*, p. 160].

However, Cohen acknowledged that his theory of middle-class delinquency "is frankly a speculative toying with possibilities."

Cohen has suggested another possibility.

Without committing ourselves . . . it is possible that the circumstances which, according to our theory, give rise to the delinquent subculture may sometimes be found in families which, *from the standpoint of purely economic criteria of social class* [emphasis in the original], would ordinarily be considered middle class. It will be remembered, however, that the most crucial elements of our explanation relate not so much to the income and the economic disadvantage of the working class as to aspects of family culture and methods of child rearing which bear a strong but by no means perfect relationship to income and occupation. We have already remarked that many families which are middle class in economic terms and live in what are known as middle-class neighborhoods may be decidedly working-class in terms of the experiences they provide their children. . . . Wherever we find the cultural conditions called for by our theory, we may expect to find the soil for the delinquent subculture. It is conceivable, then, that much of the delinquency found in "over-privileged" neighborhoods may be the same, in terms of both content and etiology, as the delinquency with which we have been concerned in this book [*ibid.*, pp. 158-159].

Cohen apparently has favored the former speculation because he has been predicting to the presence of a delinquent subculture rather than to delinquency by an individual, the first being prerequisite to the second. The latter speculation suggests that middle-class boys may be driven toward delinquency, but presumably not enough of them would be to form the basis of a continuing subculture. This writer favors the latter speculation, with some modification, and suggests that an individual boy may exhibit a pattern of delinquent behavior without contact with an established delinquent subculture.

More than any other one theory of delinquency, Cohen's has guided the course of the present research. For this reason, it will be necessary to return to it later for some modifications, especially around the problem of delinquency among higher status boys, and for a discussion of how the theory might be tested empirically. But first, other contributions to the context of this research should be explored.

The cultural anthropologist W. B. Miller (Kvaraceus and Miller, 1959) has proposed a theory similar to the culture conflict aspect of the theories of Shaw and McKay and Sutherland. Miller's theory rests on the assumption that most members of any subculture will behave according to the ideology of that subculture and that most delinquents do not deviate from the norms of the lower-class sub-culture. It goes on to identify the lower stratum of American so-ciety as a separate subculture with a distinct ideology. Primary evidence advanced for separating out the lower stratum as a sub-culture is that its modal family type is different from the higher strata family types, being mother- rather than father-centered. Family type is a common anthropological criterion for differentiating cultural groups. The ideology of the lower-class subculture, accord-ing to Miller's theory, stems largely from the prevalence of mother-centered families and includes awarding prestige to males who are tough, daring, and skilled at outsmarting others. This ideology, the theory holds, is conducive to delinquency and explains why delin-quency is more prevalent among lower status boys.

So Miller's theory argues from the culture level of social en-vironment, through the prevalent type of family group, to delinquent behavior. The theory does not explain why lower status families develop mother-centered structures but takes this as a given fact.

One of the problems with this theory is that it is doubtful that lower status individuals do not share a substantial portion of middle-class ideology. It is just at this point that Miller's theory differs sharply from Cohen's. Where Cohen has posited status deprivation as a provocation to delinquent behavior, Miller has denied that lower status boys think at all in terms of middle-class criteria. Where Cohen has interpreted delinquent behavior as specifically counter to middle-class values, Miller has asserted that middle-class values are irrelevant to the whole issue, that lower status delinquency is a positive expression of the norms of lower-class culture.

The issue ultimately boils down to whether there is in fact an isolated lower-class culture whose children are insulated from mid-dle-class values. No substantial evidence has been offered so far to support this assumption, and it may be that Miller's own recent research with a rather selected set of lower status Negro families has given rise to an overgeneralized impression.

Weakened social controls is at the core of still another theory of delinquency, this one proposed by B. Lander (1954). Lander's theory asserts that juvenile delinquency is not concentrated in lower status neighborhoods *per se*, but rather in *anomic,* or "normless" neighborhoods. According to this theory, delinquency occurs most often among people who are not so strongly bound by the norms, or rules of society, because they do not have strong ties to the society, like stable jobs, long residence in their communities, or a network of friends and relatives living around them. The residential areas containing these peripheral members of society, it is assumed, can be identified by their low rates of home ownership or by the hetrogeneity of the ethnic groups living there. Lander's data on Baltimore indicate that low rates of home ownership or fairly equal proportions of white and Negro populations in an area were more closely associated with high delinquency rates than were social status indices like housing conditions or the education level of its residents. In one sense, Lander's data provide an answer to the question of why more lower status boys are delinquent; for they also show that anomic neighborhoods are frequently lower rather than higher status.

The present study repeated Lander's finding for Flint, Michigan. It will be recalled that in Table 2, data on the relationship between status of elementary school districts and delinquency rates showed that a low proportion of home-owners was more closely associated with a high rate of delinquency than was a low value of the dwelling unit. Bordua (1959) has replicated most of Lander's findings in Detroit.

In terms of a social-psychological orientation, Lander has suggested that delinquency is a function of the relationship between the community and the individual. Some boys are not bound into their communities so tightly, and so community norms and controls have less effect on them. Lander has not specified whether or not community factors operate through small groups or directly upon individuals.

W. Reckless, S. Dinitz, and B. Kay (1957) also offered a theory which explains delinquency on the basis of weakened controls. Their theory is built around a psychological factor, self concept, which is a boy's description of himself. According to this explanation, youngsters who learn to regard themselves as "good boys" because they are rewarded for being good at home and among their peers do not become delinquents. Even in neighborhoods where there are many delinquents about, a positive self concept insulates boys from becoming delinquent themselves. On the other hand, if boys are not rewarded for "being good," and especially if they are rewarded by parents or peers for antisocial, destructive behavior, they develop self concepts conducive to delinquency. Research by Reckless, Dinitz, and Kay supports the theory. Sixth-grade boys nominated by teachers as "potential delinquents" were found more often to have negative self concepts than boys nominated as "potential non-delinquents." But the researchers did not detail how a negative self concept develops nor how it might be linked to social status. Their theorizing is limited to the effect of face-to-face groups on boys' attitudes, particularly their attitudes toward themselves.

A paper by A. J. Reiss, Jr., "Delinquency as a Failure of Personal and Social Controls" (1951), distinguishes three sources of controls over delinquency which include most of the range of the social environment as it has been differentiated in the social-psychological orientation of this research (italics mine throughout).

> A major source of a person's control lies in the social controls of the *community and its institutions* . . . control by such institutions lies in the nature and strength of the norms of the institutions and the effectiveness of the institutional rules in obtaining behavior in conformity with norms [*ibid.*, p. 201].

> *Primary groups* are the basic institutions for the development of personal controls and the exercise of social control over the child. These groups exercise social control over the non-delinquent child by providing non-delinquent social roles and by employing techniques which make non-delinquent norms and rules effective [*ibid.*, p. 198].

> It is generally assumed that the *personality* of individuals who conform to norms to which legal penalties are attached is characterized by (a) mature ego ideals or non-delinquent social roles, i.e., internalized controls of social groups governing behavior in conformity with non-delinquent group expectations, and (b) appropriate and flexible rational controls over behavior which permit conscious guidance of action in accord with non-delinquent group expectations [*ibid.*, p. 203].

Discussing community controls, Reiss invoked both culture conflict and normlessness to account for their apparent weakness in some urban areas. He wrote, "The norms of residents [of congested, run-down areas] are observed to be relatively at variance with the norms and rules of the social system and the consensus order is relatively weak and ineffective in controlling behavior" (*ibid.*, p. 201).

When Reiss discussed primary group controls, he focused on family group as the one most relevant to control. He further assumed that "an important part of family control is the ability of the family to meet the needs of its members" (*ibid.*, p. 198). Since lower status families are those having fewer economic resources, parental authority is impaired and these families are less able to establish controls. Reiss also pointed to the consequences for weakened family controls of broken families; of parents who are themselves delinquent; of overly severe, inconsistent, or lax punishment; and of complete separation from the family for institutionalization or foster home placement.

Reiss' paper is least specific at the level of personal controls. Three classifications are offered: "(a) relatively strong ego and/or super-ego controls, (b) relatively weak ego controls [immature person of low self-esteem], and (c) relatively weak super-ego controls ['social deteriorated' or 'delinquency oriented' personality]" (*ibid.*, p. 203). How boys develop these sorts of personal controls is not suggested, however. No attempt was made in the Reiss paper to link the three levels of controls.

Reiss attempted to predict recidivism from the strength of each of the three levels of control. He found that the best predictions could be made from personal controls.

> The results *suggest* [italics his] that efficient prediction is obtained when we use items as predictors which are measures of the adequacy of personal controls of the *individual and* his relation to social control in terms of the acceptance of or submission to social control. Such measures of personal and social control appear to yield more efficient prediction of delinquent recidivism than items which are measures of the strength of social control [*ibid.*, p. 206].

This is to say, in terms of the social-psychological orientation of this research, that the best predictors of repeated delinquent behavior come from the individual rather than from the social environment levels of analysis. This conclusion is consistent with the assumption made here that the causes of delinquency, as with any other behavior, must be understood in terms of the forces operating psychologically to provoke or control it.

The several explanations for delinquency which have been outlined so far have all been proposed by sociologists and anthropologists. Psychologists and psychiatrists have also concerned themselves with the problem, and while their explanations might be expected to differ from those of other disciplines, they too may be placed in the general social-psychological framework and in terms of provocations and controls.

In general, psychologists have not been concerned with provocations toward delinquency which have their source in the social environment. This may be due to the impact of psychoanalytic theory on personality psychology. According to Freud and many theorists in the psychoanalytic school, the task is not to explain why some people are destructive, but why so many are not. This formulation of the problem of antisocial deviance follows from the psychoanalytic notion that the aggressive-destructive impulse is innate to human personality and must be controlled by the social order. With this view pervading psychological thinking, it is not surprising that psychologists have focused on control factors to explain delinquency.

A. Aichhorn (1935) and F. Redl and D. Wineman (1957) represent those psychologists who have focused primarily on self-controls. That is, their explanation for delinquency rests on the idea that the elements of personality which perform the function of holding aggressive-destructive impulses in check are underdeveloped in some youngsters. These youngsters fall into two overlapping but distinguishable groups. In one group are those who have never developed the capacity to restrain themselves from impulsive behavior, although they feel what they do is wrong and feel guilty afterward; because of the anxiety which besets these youngsters in their inability to avoid guilt, they are considered neurotic. In the other group are those who have never developed the kinds of consciences which serve as a basis for self-control compatible with the social organization within which they live; their antisocial behavior is calculated and leaves little if any residue of guilt, and so these youngsters are termed "socialized" delinquents. L. E. Hewitt and R. L. Jenkins (1956) have reported a successful attempt to sort youngsters into "unsocialized" and "socialized" categories.

While researchers like Aichhorn, Redl, and Wineman have concerned themselves primarily with the internal personality dynamics of delinquents and the process of effective treatment, giving less attention to how delinquents got that way to begin with, others have focused mainly on etiology. There is general agreement among the latter group that family relationships are the important delinquency-producing factors, because according to most accepted theory in psychology, a person's family is by far the major factor in his personality development. Representative of research in this area is an investigation by W. Healy and A. F. Bronner (1936), who studied a sample of delinquents and their non-delinquent siblings. Comparing delinquents with less troublesome brothers or sisters, they concluded that disturbed relationships with parents characterized the former. Nye (*op. cit.*), a sociologist, has compared the family relationships of self-reported delinquents with those of unrelated non-delinquents and arrived at the same conclusion.

Healy's and Bronner's theory seems to emphasize provocations rather than controls. It suggests that delinquency expresses the aggression generated by frustrations in family relationships. Children whose relationships with their parents do not satisfy their needs for love turn to delinquency as an indirect expression of aggression against their parents.

A Theory of Delinquency and Social Structure: Controls

A review of previous thinking and research on delinquency revealed some of the provocations and controls which workers in the field have regarded as important. With these as leads, the initial task for this study was to construct some hypothetical processes which might link social status with delinquent behavior, processes which might then be traced empirically. More specifically, factors characteristic of the social environment of lower status boys were sought which might be transformed into attitudes conducive to delinquency; and these factors were then examined for their possible relevance to delinquency among higher status boys. This discussion will begin with controlling forces and sources of their weakness, then go on to provocations.

Control appears in the literature at several levels. At the level of culture, conceived primarily in terms of ideology, culture conflict is often invoked to explain delinquency. At the social organizational level, lack of integration into socializing institutions like schools and churches and consequent lack of consensus about what is proper behavior are supposed to dissipate controls. At the small group level, contact with delinquent groups and the failure of the family to establish societal controls are projected as reasons for weakened controls. All of these factors have been theoretically related in some way to social status. In the present work, two processes were selected for exploration, one linking community factors to delinquent behavior; the other beginning at the cultural level and tracing links through the community, then the family, and finally to control over the delinquent boy. While these two processes are independent in their effects, they share a key concept, *attraction*, upon which are based hypotheses about control.

It was assumed that an important determinant of one individual's control over another, or the control of a group or social organization over an individual depends heavily on the attractiveness of the controlling individual or social organization to the control target. To the extent that an individual wants to have a positive relationship with another individual, group, or social organization, he will submit to their influence, agreeing with their standards and behaving as they would like him to behave. If such attraction does not bind the person to another, control or influence of the other over him is apt to be weak.

A great deal of research on individual and group sources of control supports the assumption of the importance of attraction. On the individual level, social-psychologist T. M. Newcomb and his associates have hypothesized and demonstrated the relationship between attraction and control (Newcomb, 1953; McGrath, 1955). They find that individuals are more often influenced by others whom they regard as friends. On the group level, it has been found that individuals are more often influenced by the standards of groups to which they are attracted (cf. Back, 1951; Cartwright, 1951; Festinger, Schachter, and Back, 1950). Often this relationship is put in terms of "group cohesiveness" which is defined as "the sum of members' attractions to the group." The concept of attraction has not been used explicitly by researchers at the level of larger social organizations; but discussions like Landers' (*op. cit.*) of the conditions which generate *anomie,* which describes a situation of weakened social controls, emphasize lack of integration into a community, church, and so forth. This lack of integration may be indicative of lack of opportunity to become part of a social institution, but lack of attraction to social institutions may really underlie *anomic* conditions.

Social organizations do not always need to rely on attraction to achieve control, but the condition under which attraction is *not* important seldom occurs in the context of delinquent behavior by adolescent boys in a normal community. This condition exists when the social organization can apply such coercive force that the person must submit, and escape is difficult or impossible. In this condition, control over the individual's behavior is established whether or not he is attracted to the social organization. But it is reasonable to suppose that this condition does not exist for adolescent boys in Flint. It seems unlikely, for example, that police are a major source of coercive control over juvenile delinquency, especially compared to potential attractiveness of families and community; for police could not be expected to maintain the kind of surveillance over youth which would be necessary to deter delinquency effectively. Police function largely to remove the most visible community and family failures, perhaps occasionally to give other individuals or institutions a chance to establish the attraction necessary to achieve control.

With the dependency of control upon attraction as an assumption, the next theoretical step was to suggest some of the class-linked sources of attraction which might promote control over adolescent boys. These were sought in the *community* and in the *family* The hypotheses which were developed are discussed only briefly here and expanded upon in later chapters where the data testing them are presented.

It was supposed that the Flint community would be attractive to boys to the extent that it met some of their salient needs. Those needs which the community might be expected to meet center about recreation, education, and the opportunity for making a respectable living in the future. Of course, education and future opportunity are closely related; for one of the criteria for the worth of education is its relevance to future jobs. Nevertheless, both recreational and educational facilities can be evaluated independently in terms of the quality of the facilities. It is suggested here that *the higher the quality of recreational and educational facilities, the more attractive the community will be to its youngsters, and consequently, the less likely they will be delinquent.* This hypothesis covers two levels in a process from community facilities to delinquency. The first link is the relationship between the quality of facilities and boys' attitude toward the community, a link here called *attraction.* The second link is the relationship between attraction and the likelihood of boys becoming delinquent, the link called *control.*

In order to accomplish the aim of this research, however, another link must be added to the hypothetical process-chain, which joins it to social status. The link between the quality of recreational and educational facilities on the one hand and social status on the other seems clear. *It is expected that the quality of recreational and educational facilities will be poorer in lower status neighborhoods.* If this is true, then conditions are more detrimental to social control among lower than among higher status boys. This might help to explain the greater participation of the former in delinquency.

The family is the key control link in the second process-chain considered. The family was brought into the framework of the present work by assuming it and its separate members were subject to the same attraction-control dynamics as any other group or individual. The attractiveness of a family group, like the attractiveness of a community, depends upon the extent to which it meets a son's needs. A family is expected to satisfy an almost infinite variety of needs, ranging from providing essentials like food, clothing, and love, to offering perhaps the less essential but still crucial family car on a Saturday night. This research could not be expected to measure the extent to which each family satisfied all its son's needs. Special attention was paid, however, to a boy's father as a potentially attractive, and consequently controlling figure. Psychoanalytic theory on the source of a boy's conscience led to this emphasis. According to psychoanalytic thinking, conscience is established through identification with the like-sexed parent in the early years of life, and this identifying process is recapitulated at adolescence. The period of recapitulation was a focus of this study, under the assumption that identification breakdown at adolescence is important to the delinquency phenomenon.

Many factors probably affect a boy's feelings about his father as a person with whom to identify; that is, as one with whom he feels he shares attitudes and interests, as a person whom he does

or would like to resemble.   Limits had to be set on which factors
would be studied, and the central concern of this study dictated that
status-linked factors had priority.   Two possibilities were explored:
father as an image of "the successful man" and father as "the head
of the family."

Insofar as the success image is important in a father's attractiveness to his son, cultural definitions of "success" immediately
disadvantage the lower status father as an object of emulation.   A
lower status father has to overcome the social evaluation of the
"clean" and "dirty" job and the men who hold them in order to gain
his son's respect.   Most of the images of "father" current in American society and presented to boys in their earliest readers and in
television and movie portrayals of family life are the fathers of
perhaps the 20 per cent highest status boys, fathers home from offices to houses with picture windows looking out, and in, on better
parts of town.   It may be that a low status father's effectiveness in
controlling his son is impaired by his status in the community.   Not
only will his direct attempts to guide his son's behavior fail, but
also he will fail to become a potent part of the abiding inner voice
which could deter his son from delinquency.

Another basis for a father's attractiveness to his son may be
the father's influence over family decisions in general.   Family
members have different degrees of influence in their family group,
a fact acknowledged in expressions like "wearing the pants in the
family" and "the hen-pecked husband."   It is suggested here that a
father's position in his family, especially his influence relative to
his wife's, is a factor in whether his son is attracted to him and
thus amenable to his control.

The influence men exert in their families, compared to their
wives' influence, is in part determined by their status in the community.   There seem to be images current of the working-class man
who dominates his household and the middle-class man who shares
decisions with his wife if he does not surrender them to her alto-
gether.   The present work proceeds on the hypothesis that the reverse is true, that higher status fathers are more influential.   There
are fairly firm grounds, theoretical and empirical, for the assertion
that lower status husbands usually wield less power in their families
vis-à-vis their wives than do higher status husbands.   These grounds
are explored in a later chapter where findings are presented about
family aspects of control over delinquency.

Finally, parents will not be effective in keeping their sons
from becoming delinquent if they are themselves delinquent.   Being

controlled by another implies controls against delinquency only if the other upholds social standards. As Sutherland's theory of differential association points out, delinquency may be encouraged by contact with criminal elements. In fact, the McCords (1958) gathered data which demonstrated that sons of criminals were more often delinquent than sons of law-abiding citizens. People other than family members who do not uphold community norms also may prove detrimental to social control over the behavior of boys.

A Theory of Delinquency and Social Structure: Provocations

Essentially two kinds of provocations to delinquency have appeared in the literature, the innate aggressive-destructive impulse and the motive for status. It is interesting that the provocations of poverty have not been suggested as a cause for delinquency. It seems reasonable to suppose, for example, that lower status boys will steal to get things which are denied them because their parents cannot afford to give them much. But the best data available indicate that poverty is probably not a major provocation. If poverty were a major provocation to delinquency, one would expect delinquency rates to go up in times of unemployment and depression and down in times of prosperity. In fact, the opposite is true (Glaser and Rice, 1959; Reineman, 1947; Laird, 1933; Stermer, 1936). The rise in rates during periods of prosperity suggests that status is an important provocation, for it is during prosperous times that prestige symbols of money and power may be most sought after.

The innate aggressive-destructive impulse was not studied in the present research. Because psychoanalytic theory asserts that this impulse is universal in human nature, it cannot be directly linked to social structure and so is not central to our concern here. But it should be pointed out that if this provocation indeed turns out to be central to delinquency, the reasons for lower status boys more often becoming delinquent will have to depend solely on differences in social control.

Status deprivation is a provocation intimately linked to social status on the one hand and delinquency on the other. Following Cohen's theory, status deprivation here means failure to obtain the wealth and power which are the main criteria by which social strata are ordered. For boys, placement in a social structure is almost always the same as getting a job of a particular status. So status deprivation for boys may be considered anticipated failure to get a prestigeful job. One of the tasks for this research was to isolate

some of the factors in a boy's present social status which determined his perception of the kind of job he is likely to fill as an
adult.

Two factors were explored. First, there was a search for
indications of class-consciousness, an attempt to discover if boys
felt that social class beginnings in themselves determined life chances.
For this reason, boys and their parents were asked about their belief in The American Dream of equal opportunity. Second, the potency of personal attributes was tested for their part in determining
perceived life chances. Earlier in this chapter Cohen was quoted
as he pointed out that perceived personal shortcomings may determine a boy's estimation of his future. Specifically, a boy's performance in school may signal for him the chances he has of becoming a "success." The school in American society is an important way up. Warner, Havighurst, and Loeb, in their book *Who Shall
Be Educated?* (1954), present the image of education as a conveyor
belt carrying youngsters upward and onward through the social system. They point out that social class is an important determinant
of who gets off where, but ability is also a factor. The point here
is that ability may be a very important factor to the boys themselves, regardless of its actual potency.

Links between social status and status deprivation are apparent. Class-consciousness, of course, would create greater feelings
of status deprivation among lower compared to higher status boys.
As far as school achievement is concerned, it has been clearly established that lower status boys are more likely to perform poorly
in school (cf. Sexton, 1960; D. C. Shaw, 1943).

The last link, from status deprivation to delinquency, is an
especially important one because status deprivation is more specific
to delinquency than any of the control factors discussed. Weakened
controls leave paths open to deviancy of many sorts; any of the
standards of the weak group or individual may be violated. The
consequences of weakened controls need not be increased violation
of legal norms, that is, delinquency. But status deprivation in theory provokes boys particularly to delinquent acts. Cohen has suggested that delinquency is a double solution to the problem of status
deprivation: It overthrows the values whose attainment is blocked
and at the same time it adds to the status of a boy among his delinquent peers.

Summary of Hypotheses

I. Social status, attraction, control, and delinquency
  A. Community variables
      Hypothesis 1: Recreational and educational facilities will be differentially distributed in a community so that lower status boys have poorer facilities available to them.
      Hypothesis 2: The quality of recreational and educational facilities in different neighborhoods of the community will be related to the attitudes toward the community of boys living in different neighborhoods, so that boys with poorer facilities available to them will be less attracted to the community.
      Hypothesis 3: Since attraction is the primary basis of social control, boys who are less attracted to their community will more likely be delinquent.

It follows from these three hypotheses that lower status boys will more likely be delinquent. However, the implication of Hypothesis 3 is that the less *any* boy is attracted to his community, the more likely he will be delinquent, whether he is higher or lower status. That is, relatively low attraction to the community is expected to characterize higher and lower status delinquents alike.

  B. Family variables
      Hypothesis 4: The status of a man's job in his society will be related to the amount of influence he wields in his family, so that lower status men are less influential.
      Hypothesis 5a: A son's attraction to his father is related to the influence the father wields in his family, so that the less influential boys perceive their fathers to be, the less they will be attracted to them.
      Hypothesis 5b: A son's attraction to his father is related directly to the status of his father's job in his society, so that the lower the status of fathers' jobs, the less attractive fathers will be to their sons.
      Hypothesis 6: Since attraction is the primary basis of social control, and since fathers are primary sources of social control for adolescent boys: the less boys are attracted to their fathers, the more likely they will be delinquent.

It follows from Hypotheses 4 through 6 that lower status boys will more likely be delinquent. However, the implication of Hypothesis 6 is that relatively low attraction to father characterizes higher and lower status delinquents alike.

II. Social status, provocation, and delinquency
    A. Class consciousness variables
        Hypothesis 7: Belief in The American Dream of equality of opportunity is differentially distributed among boys in different social statuses, so that fewer lower status boys believe in The American Dream.
        Hypothesis 8: Since anticipation of occupational failure creates problems of status deprivation which delinquency is especially suited to solve, lower status boys who do not believe in The American Dream are more likely to become delinquent.
    B. Personal failure variables
        Hypothesis 9: School achievement is related to social status, so that lower status boys do less well in school.
        Hypothesis 10: Since the level of school achievement is a cue to future occupational success, boys who do less well in school will more likely anticipate occupational failure.
        Hypothesis 11: Since anticipation of occupational failure creates problems of status deprivation which delinquency is especially suited to solve, boys who do less well in school are more likely to become delinquent.

It follows from Hypotheses 7 through 11 that lower status boys will more likely be delinquent. However, the implications of Hypotheses 10 and 11 are that anticipation of occupational failure, prompted for example by poor performance in school, provokes delinquency among higher and lower status boys alike.

Chapter III

RESEARCH STRATEGY

Studies of juvenile delinquency have often run afoul of methodological problems which cast doubt on their conclusions. Some researchers have neglected to include non-delinquent comparison groups so that it is impossible to tell if their findings really distinguish delinquents from non-delinquents. Others have included comparison groups, but they have been different from the delinquent groups in other important ways besides incidence of delinquency. For example, comparison groups have been chosen from a different social stratum than the delinquents so that differences between delinquent and non-delinquent groups might be due to social status rather than delinquency. Still other researchers have chosen youngsters to study as delinquents without being clear about what criteria were used to determine delinquency.

The design of this research was built as far as was possible on the experiences of previous researchers. An attempt was made to choose delinquent groups according to clear and reasonable criteria. A comparison group was chosen so that whatever differences were found would most probably be attributed to differences in delinquency. Research instruments included a variety of tools, from measures of delinquency rates to individual projective tests, in order to measure variables as directly as possible. The final design still is not foolproof, but it seems to come close enough to justify drawing conclusions about the hypotheses tested.

This chapter and the next describe the research design, the setting in which it was effected, and the major instruments employed.

The Research Site: Flint, Michigan

Flint was chosen as a research site for several reasons. In the first place, it seemed desirable to study delinquency some place other than in the deteriorated areas of the largest American cities. Most studies of delinquency have been done in such settings, and for that reason represent studies of the most visible and perhaps the most distinctive forms of delinquency. Another look at the problem was necessary, one which focused on delinquency not associated with miserable slums, depressed minorities, virulent gang warfare, and so forth. A decision was made to study delinquency as it might develop under conditions more prevalent throughout the United States.

A related reason for selecting Flint was that juvenile crime was not an exceptional problem there. Although Flint citizens are concerned about any number of juvenile delinquents, certainly delinquency has not nearly approached the incidence or virulence there as has been reported for parts of New York City, Chicago, or Detroit. Comparison of delinquency rates in one city to rates elsewhere must be a cautious practice, because the figures are gathered in so many different ways and police practices themselves vary so widely from city to city. But, with this caution in mind, the figures in Table 4, on delinquency rates in selected Michigan counties for 1957, show that the rate in Genessee County, which Flint dominates, was neither the highest nor the lowest in Michigan, compared to those of other counties which include medium to large cities.

A third reason for selecting Flint was its receptivity to research. The city has a host of research efforts in its history, including Carr's (1957) research on delinquency in the '30's and the work of the Flint Area Study, a multi-faceted research project of The University of Michigan's Department of Sociology. In addition, Flint has been especially sensitive to problems of youth and for this reason encouraged the establishment of a Flint Youth Study.

Flint is a medium-sized city of 200,000, the largest in Michigan after Detroit, which is fifty miles south. The city as a whole is a sudden cluster of buildings on rolling Michigan countryside. The buildings are almost exclusively one or two stories high, except for a short stretch of Saginaw Street, main stem of the downtown business district, where a few office buildings and department stores stand higher.

Flint's economy is dominated by General Motors. Almost half its labor force is on a General Motors payroll; two-thirds of its factory employees work in General Motors plants. The three next largest Flint industries supply General Motors with paints, iron castings, and fabrics respectively. When Americans don't buy Buicks or Chevrolets, homes-for-sale ads take a full page in the Flint *Journal* and stores fail on Saginaw Street. So Flint's history since 1900 is largely the history of the world's largest corporation; Flint's present is also intimately linked to the fortunes of General Motors; and its

Table 4

The rate of juvenile delinquency in Flint is neither high nor low
compared to the rates in other Michigan cities with populations
over 50,000.[a]

County	Major City	1957 Juvenile Court Delinquency Rate per 1,000 Children
Kalamazoo	Kalamazoo	8.5
Muskegon	Muskegon	6.2
Calhoun	Battle Creek	4.8
Oakland	Pontiac-Royal Oak	4.8
Saginaw	Saginaw	4.1
Washtenaw	Ann Arbor	4.0
GENESEE	FLINT	3.8
Wayne	Detroit	3.8
Kent	Grand Rapids	3.6
Macomb	Detroit suburbs	3.5
Jackson	Jackson	1.9
Ingham	Lansing-East Lansing	1.8

a. Source: State Department of Social Welfare, *Michigan Juvenile Court Reporting, 1957*.

future in all likelihood will continue to be. It is to be expected that
when one talks to a Flint boy about his town and about his future
employment, one evokes the image of an automobile plant.

When this study was in the field, roughly from November, 1957
to May, 1958, cars were not selling well, and Flint was for a time
declared an "economic disaster area" by the Federal government,
when its unemployment rate climbed to a peak of 18 per cent. Interviewers frequently found fathers home during weekday mornings
and afternoons when, under ordinary conditions, interviewing adult
males is largely an evening and weekend employment. Economic
conditions in Flint during the course of data collection should be kept
in mind when interpreting the findings. While they probably did not
affect the differences found between delinquents and non-delinquents

and their families, since they were the same for both groups, poor economic conditions may have had some effects on the general level of responses concerning community attractiveness, job futures, and such.

There were no flourishing teen-age gangs in Flint in 1957 or since. One gang, the "Leather Jacket Gang," had been uncovered in 1953 and seemed to disintegrate when a few of its alleged leaders were sent to Boys Vocational School in Lansing. But even this gang, according to the Juvenile Bureau of the Flint Police Department, looked larger than it really was because lots of boys who were not members sported leather jackets for effect in the gang's heyday. When the effect grew to be more negative than positive in an aroused and reacting community, the jackets were left at home.

Furthermore the kinds of delinquent behaviors exhibited in Flint are similar to the pattern of delinquency in most places. Table 5 presents the figures on relative incidences of different types

Table 5

Percentages of court cases by offense for the city of Flint and for the state of Michigan (1957).

Offense	Michigan[a] (per cent) (N = 10,197)	Flint[b] (per cent) (N = 137)
Auto stealing	14	18
Other stealing	39	35
Injury to person	5	16
Damage to property	7	1
Carelessness or mischief	6	5
Running away	5	2
Incorrigible or disobedient	9	—
Sex offense	4	2
Truancy	6	2
Other delinquency	5	19

a. Source: *Michigan Juvenile Court Reporting*, 13th Annual Issue, 1957, Michigan Department of Social Welfare.
b. Source: Basic tables of police contact with juveniles, Flint, Michigan, 1955-57, The University of Michigan, Institute for Social Research (mimeographed).

of juvenile crime in Flint and in Michigan. In short, juvenile delinquency in Flint is probably no more nor less of a problem, nor different in character from most other urban American communities.

What delinquency there is in Flint is officially handled first by the Juvenile Bureau, a department of police, to which youth 16 or under are referred. Referrals include neglect and dependency cases as well as misdemeanors and felonies. Any officer on the Flint force might initially apprehend a delinquent youth, but if the youth becomes subject to any further police action, he is referred to the Juvenile Bureau, which thereupon takes over the case. If a case to be investigated is known to involve juveniles, a Juvenile Bureau detective usually will participate.

The different stages in the official process through which a detected delinquent might go were described in Chapter I. It is important to point out here, however, that the records of this process, while they belong officially to the Probate Court, are kept in the Juvenile Bureau. It was through the cooperation of the Court and the Bureau that this study could compile delinquency rates by Flint neighborhoods and could select a sample of juvenile delinquents to study more intensively.

One more feature of the Flint community will round out this brief description. Flint provides a great variety of special youth-centered services for a city of its size. These include large community centers; a health clinic; special school rooms for the physically and mentally handicapped; a planetarium; "community school" programs which utilize school facilities through the evening hours; two separate summer playground recreation programs; a summer camp; city-wide "Big Brother" and "Big Sister" programs; an annual Science Fair; and an opportunity to receive four years of low-tuition, high-quality college education in the community. These are possible in large part through exceptional community awareness of youth and eagerness to meet youth needs. This community support was in turn developed largely through the efforts of the Mott Foundation, which was endowed by the largest single personal stockholder in General Motors, and which among other things contributes about 8 per cent of the total Flint Board of Education budget.

The services of representatives of leading community youth agencies were lent to the research project advisory board; Flint citizens came forward to serve as interviewers; data were made available wherever and whenever the various agencies had them; agencies strongly and publicly endorsed the study while at the same time exercising no control over it (which, it should be pointed out, makes the study staff alone responsible for any errors it may have made in research or human relations). In general, the community made research possible in the often sensitive area of juvenile delinquency.

Organization of the Research Team

The staff for the research project was organized under the title Flint Youth Study. The project has been a part of a wider Program on Children, Youth and Family Life of the Institute for Social Research at The University of Michigan, under the joint direction of Dr. Ronald Lippitt, of the Institute's Research Center for Group Dynamics, and Dr. Stephen Withey of the Institute's Survey Research Center. Before beginning the work reported here, the Flint Youth Study had spent a year investigating the differences between the life conditions of Flint boys who were school behavior problems and boys who were outstanding school citizens. Since the accomplishment of the present study's field work on Caucasian male delinquents in its second year, the Flint Youth Study has gone on to investigate delinquency among females and among Negro male delinquents, and to study the cultures of youth groups, and of the set of adults who shape the policies of Flint's youth-serving agencies. The project has been supported by a series of grants from the U.S. Department of Health, Education, and Welfare, through its National Institute of Mental Health.

Measures of Community Variables

Field work for the second-year study of Caucasian male delinquents began in September, 1957, with a two-purpose use of the contact files of the Juvenile Bureau, Flint Police Department. On the one hand, Charles Seashore began the process of transferring the entire file back to January, 1955, onto punched cards for electronic computing machine analysis. This was the work which yielded three years of delinquency rates for each Flint elementary school district. Elementary school districts were chosen as "neighborhood" units since it was apparent that in Flint, and probably in other cities of its size, the elementary school district is the smallest administrative area homogeneous as to social status. The rates were figured on an annual basis, with each boy counted only once each year for the neighborhood in which he lived, and only if he committed some misdemeanor or felony other than traffic offenses. The base population on which a rate was computed was the number of boys or girls in an elementary school district according to the school census taken in April and May of each year. Since the relative positions of delinquency rates of neighborhoods proved quite stable from year to year, the rate for only the year of the study, 1957, has been cited in this report.

Delinquency rates were used in two ways, to determine their relationship to social status, and to determine their relationship to the quality of recreational and educational facilities in the various elementary school districts. Chapter I includes a report of the first investigation, along with a description of the method of determining the social status of each school district.

The quality of Flint recreational facilities was determined through data compiled by Lawrence Kersten. Unknown to the Flint Youth Study staff at the beginning of this research, Kersten, a city administration student at The University of Michigan, was performing a detailed study of public recreational facilities in Flint. The methods he used will be described in more detail when the findings are discussed; it will only be mentioned here that Kersten's work produced a quantitative index of quality with distinct components, which went far beyond the Flint Youth Study's original aspirations for data in this area.

The quality of school facilities was determined by data provided by the Flint Public Schools. These data included the age of schools, class loads, teachers' experience and degree levels, and faculty resignation figures. More detail and recreation and education data and findings concerning them are presented in Chapter V.

Selection of a Sample to Interview

While Seashore was turning contact files into punched card files, Estelle Antell, Flint Youth Study field office chief, was searching these files for delinquents to include in the "core sample." The core sample is the sample of boys, their fathers, and their mothers who were interviewed in order to measure family group and attitudinal variables. The goal was to select two different populations of delinquents, those who might be called "repeated" delinquents and those who might be called "sometime" delinquents. A repeated delinquent was a boy whose behavior indicated that his delinquency was an integral part of his life pattern, rather than a thoughtless lark at which he happened to be caught. The lark described the behavior of the sometime delinquent.

In choosing the sample of repeated and sometime delinquents, other criteria were also invoked. In order to simplify the design, *only Caucasian boys* were selected; the study of Negro delinquents would wait. Only *boys within the normal range of intelligence,* with I.Q.'s above 79, were selected to insure that the delinquency was knowledgeable at least in this respect, and also to avoid special interviewing problems. For similar reasons, *only boys over 12* were used, and, of course, Michigan state law dictated that they be *16 or under* to qualify as juveniles and have records in the Juvenile Bureau file; research interests in occupational aspirations and expectancies and the knowledge that most delinquent boys were in their teens were other reasons for electing to study boys over 12. The fact that the study worked through Flint public schools to interview boys means that some Catholic boys attending parochial schools were not selected.

Once all the boys who fit the criteria were drawn from the contact files, it was decided to place in the repeated delinquent category all the boys selected *who had committed at least two fairly serious crimes within the three years previous.* This criterion for distinguishing repeated delinquents was indicated by the minority of boys, about 38 per cent, who committed a second offense. It marked off even the one-time repeater as a special case and still allowed for enough boys in the repeated category on which to apply research statistics. In fact, only about half of the repeated delinquents had but two contacts on his record, as Table 6 shows.

By "serious crime" is meant delinquency other than traffic violations, truancy, "carry BB guns within city limits," and the like.

Table 6

About half of the repeated delinquents had a record of only two previous police contacts; the rest had longer records.

Number of Police Contacts on Record	Number of Boys	Per Cent of Boys
2	48	52
3	18	19
4	11	12
5+	16	17
Total	93	100

Delinquents in this study are boys who committed robberies, assaults, arson, and such. If later interviewing showed clearly that the police contact was in error, that the boy was not actually guilty of the suspected crime, the boy was not included in data analysis.

A sometime delinquent is *a boy who committed a serious crime only once in the previous three years*. He fit all the other criteria of a repeated delinquent except for the number of crimes he committed, plus one additional criterion: *he had to have lived in Flint for at least three years* to ensure that he had not piled up a longer police record elsewhere.

It might be supposed that a few of the sometime delinquents were actually repeated delinquents who either didn't get caught the other times, or hadn't yet had time to express their delinquent patterns fully. It was precisely because of these possibilities that sometime delinquents were chosen for study, for these boys could then be used to check the findings in two ways. First, if the sometime delinquents were in fact a mixture of mostly non-delinquents and some undetected or incipient repeated delinquents, they would reveal life patterns which as a group place them between non-delinquents and repeated delinquents; that is, the repeated delinquent boys hidden in the sometimes category should have added delinquency-related elements to the picture presented in the data by the total sometime category. Second, some of those sometime delinquents who were "at heart" repeated delinquents should have revealed themselves by more delinquent behavior within a year or so after initial interviewing, when a follow-up search was made of the police files. These boys, now clearly repeated delinquents, and their families, should have in their earlier interviews presented a picture more like that of the original group of repeated delinquents than like their own group of sometime delinquents. Data were analyzed to see if sometime delinquents did behave as a category between the non-delinquents and the repeated delinquents, and if boys who later repeated had responded differently from boys who did not repeat; the results of this analysis are presented in Chapter VIII, where they bear on the direction of the causal process in delinquency.

Selected for comparison purposes was a sample of "non-delinquents," boys who fit all criteria met by repeated and sometime delinquents except that they had no record whatsoever in the Juvenile Bureau files, for any sort of misdemeanor or felony. If it was later discovered through interviewing that a boy did have a record with another law enforcement agency, like the State Police, he was dropped from the study.

The non-delinquents were selected from a sample of boys attending Flint's junior and senior public high schools. The secretaries in the various school offices were asked to select rooms in which research staff members might distribute blanks to boys requesting information about name, age, address, presence of parents at home, and parents' occupations. The blanks were filled out in class. Information about race, I.Q., and police record was added afterward. On the basis of information on these blanks, non-delinquents were matched one-for-one with repeated delinquents. All were matched for race, since only Caucasians were included. In addition, a non-delinquent was within 10 points of I.Q. and within 12 months of age of the repeated delinquent member of his pair. Both boys attended the same level school, either junior or senior high school. Their fathers worked at occupations not more than one U.S. census category apart, so that a factory operative's son might be matched with a foreman's son but not with a lawyer's, and a plant manager's son with a minister's son but not with a spot welder's; in actuality, most of the occupation matches were within the same census category. Ninety-three pairs of non-delinquents and repeated delinquents were established.

Half of these pairs became triplets, by adding to each a sometime delinquent who met the same matching criteria for both the non-delinquent and repeated delinquent members of the pair to which he was assigned. It was because of the difficulty of this double matching procedure that only 43 of the pairs became triplets, but it was decided to be rigorous about matching and sacrifice a larger sample.

For a closer look at the matched core sample, the reader is referred to the detailed list in Appendix I.

Since the central concern of this research was to investigate delinquent behavior as it developed in separate social strata, it was necessary to identify these strata among the boys selected. For reasons outlined in Chapter I, father's occupation was the fact which determined social status for a boy, or the occupation of the major family breadwinner if there was no father at home. The sample was divided into three strata: white collar, skilled workers, and semi- or unskilled workers, as these are identified by census categories. The white collar category includes a broad range of occupations, from salesclerk to lawyer. The other two categories are narrower, skilled workers being foremen, craftsmen, and the like, while semi- and unskilled workers include machine operators, truck drivers, construction laborers, and such.

Table A-1 (Appendix II) presents the resulting "core sample," including the numbers of fathers and mothers who were interviewed in each category. Fewer parents than boys were interviewed because in some cases, a father or mother was no longer part of a boy's family, through death or separation, and because in a few cases, a parent refused to respond to an interview. Nine fathers and eight mothers declined to be interviewed, about half of them parents of repeated delinquents.

Parents were able to provide more information about their social backgrounds than boys reliably knew, so responses by parents concerning income, education, and place of origin presents a fuller picture of the similarities and differences between the delinquent and non-delinquent portions of the core sample.

Some differences in social backgrounds can be noted. Although delinquents and non-delinquents were carefully matched according to their fathers' occupations, greater proportions of repeated delinquents' families were in the highest and lowest income brackets (see Table A-2). The average income of the two groups are about the same. The education level achieved by fathers is about the same in the three groups, while the repeated delinquents' mothers are slightly less well-educated on the whole than the rest (see Table A-3). There are no outstanding differences in the sections of the country where parents grew up; but the fathers of repeated delinquents more often grew up in small towns than did the fathers of non-delinquents, who more often grew up in large cities (see Table A-4).

It is difficult to know how these social background differences might have compounded with delinquent-non-delinquent comparisons to be presented later to produce results which then cannot be attributed really to the differences in delinquency, or how these differences might have masked differences between delinquents and non-delinquents. A few repeated delinquent versus non-delinquent comparisons were made, controlling on these aspects of social backgrounds, with no significant change in the findings. It is likely that they are not operating to overcome the delinquency factor in comparisons.

Interview Procedure

Most of the boys were interviewed at school by college men. Each school cooperated by providing a room where a boy and the staff interviewer could talk alone for an hour or more. Some of the boys were interviewed at home because they could not be found at school, having formally or informally dropped out. Still a few others were interviewed at institutions for juvenile offenders in Flint or elsewhere. One boy was finally located and interviewed in a bowling alley. Every boy originally selected whose home address was still in the Flint area was eventually interviewed.

At another session, boys responded to paper-and-pencil questionnaires with the group of boys interviewed at his school.

Parents were usually interviewed at home, mothers by women and fathers by men. Efforts were made to keep the interviews private, but in about half the cases, other family members popped in and out during the sessions which lasted from a little under one to well over two hours. In some cases, interviews were held at places of business, in parked cars, at neighborhood restaurants, and in bars.

The study was introduced to boys and parents as a study of youth, not specifically of delinquency. In most cases, interviewers did not initially know if the respondent was a delinquent boy or not, or the parent of a delinquent boy. Interviewers picked up the name and address of their assignment at the field office and were asked not to interview anyone whom they knew personally. But some interviewers spotted delinquents by figuring out the office's coding system. In many cases, the fact of a boy's delinquency became apparent very shortly after an interview began. In any case, interviewers had been trained to stick very closely to the prepared set of questions comprising the interview schedule and to depart from it when necessary only with neutral explanations and questions. Interviewers were also trained to record respondents' statements verbatim, making no interpretations of their own unless they were clearly labeled interpretations.

Completed interviews were logged in at the field office and then transmitted to the Study office at the Institute for Social Research in Ann Arbor. These interviews were "content analyzed"; that is, professional coders cast the answers to interview questions into predetermined categories. A random sample representative of all the interviews was analyzed separately by two people whose agreement would insure that the categorization of responses was not merely arbitrary but accurately represented the sense of what respondents had said. The categorizations on which the data reported here are based were agreed upon more than 90 per cent of the time. Categorized information was then punched onto electronic computer cards in preparation for data analysis.

Some Important Features of the Research Method

Some aspects of the strategy of this research should be singled out for discussion.   The first of these is the use of detected delinquents, rather than court cases or, as has been more usual in delinquency research, institutionalized youngsters.   The use of detected delinquents is especially crucial in an investigation of family background factors in delinquency.   The family backgrounds of court cases and institutionalized delinquents very likely represent a special selection of the families of boys who are apprehended for delinquent behavior because, as was pointed out in Chapter I, boys are probably referred to courts and sent to institutions largely on account of atypical family backgrounds which result in ineffective control.   To find that the families of institutionalized delinquents are broken or destitute or antisocial or just generally unattractive may not be a finding about delinquent boys' families generally, but a finding confirming the judgments of the officials who institutionalized a certain small proportion of the delinquents they handled.   By studying detected delinquents irrespective of later disposition, it was possible to get a more nearly accurate picture of the families of boys who commit delinquent acts.   Table 7 shows how many repeated and sometime delinquents were merely contacted, how many were booked, how many referred to the Probate Court, and how many were institutionalized.   Later on, data will be presented on variables related to the family life of delinquents compared to non-delinquents.   It should be noted here that the findings to be reported hold for delinquents regardless of the disposition of their cases.

Table 7

The official disposition of the cases which make up repeated delinquent and sometime delinquent samples.

	Contacted; Only	Contacted; Booked	Contacted; Booked; Referred to Court	Contacted; Booked Referred to Court; Institutionalized
Repeated Delinquents	24% (N=22)	13% (12)	52% (48[a])	12% (11)
Sometime Delinquents	49% (N=21)	30% (13)	21[b]% (9[b])	0%

a. Dismissed: 24 per cent; N = 22.   Probated: 28 per cent; N = 26.
b. Dismissed: 21 per cent; N = 9.   Probated: 0 per cent; N = 0.

It is important to note that boys, mothers, and fathers were themselves interviewed, rather than relying on boys to report their parents' attitudes, another common practice. Too often, it was felt, boys' perceptions of their parents' attitudes would be distorted by lack of information or by emotional elements. Such distortion might be especially crucial in an investigation of delinquency. By interviewing boys and their parents separately, it was possible to use distortion as a known variable for study, rather than leaving it as an unknown source of error.

Matching boys one-for-one, on the basis of their fathers' occupations helped a great deal to control the social status factor. Previous studies such as the Gluecks' (1950), which matched boys on the basis of their neighborhoods as a social status index, have ended up with samples in which delinquents' families are, by income or education measures obtained in later interviews, actually of much lower status than their non-delinquent matches.

In the present design, the one-for-one matching procedure was utilized at the stage of data analysis as well. These techniques will be described when they become relevant to understanding tables of data later. Here it is only pointed out that when an item of data was missing from a particular boy or parent, the corresponding information obtained from the matched respondent was then discarded.

The next chapter consists of parallel records of responses obtained from a pair of boys and their parents, which will enable the reader to become more familiar with the nature of the data to be reported.

Some Limitations of the Research Design

This chapter will close with a brief discussion of what kinds of statements might legitimately be made on the basis of the research design described. First of all, it is hard to say to what extent the delinquents studied here represent *all* delinquents. Strictly speaking, to represent all delinquents, they would have had to be a random sample of all delinquents. But the delinquents studied here are not even representative of Flint delinquents in the statistical sense. They are representative of other delinquents only to the extent that they are "typical," and their typicality can only be ascertained by the extent to which their behavior is like the behavior of delinquents studied elsewhere and reported about in the literature. Where comparisons with other studies were possible, they were made and are reported where relevant.

Because of this problem of representativeness, statements which begin "Delinquents are more . . ." are probably not legitimate interpretations of present findings. Rather, statements have been restricted to the form, "The repeated delinquents studied here, compared to the non-delinquents, more often. . . ." Where statements depart from this form, it is for reasons of readability; this form is always implied.

For the same reason of sample selection, statements comparing different social statuses are not strictly legitimate. The white collar families in this study, for example, are not representative of all white collar people anywhere. White collar families which include repeated delinquents are an especially peculiar set; families of non-delinquent boys may be more nearly representative, but even they are not, strictly speaking. So statements which begin, "White collar fathers are . . ." are not legitimate here. Since no matching was done across social status categories, even statements beginning "Skilled workers more than unskilled workers are . . ." are not legitimate. Nevertheless, from time to time differences in responses from one social status category to another suggested interpretations of the data, and with reservations in mind, these interpretations have been discussed. Again, where data from other studies are relevant, especially from studies of representative samples of social strata, they have been cited.

One last point should be made. Undoubtedly some of the boys categorized as "non-delinquents" have committed one or more delinquent acts which remained undetected. In fact, during the follow-up search of contact files made a year or so after the initial interviewing phase and after all the initial data were analyzed, two non-delinquents did prove to be delinquents whose records were somehow overlooked in the first screening process. But nevertheless, this can be said with confidence: the non-delinquent category must be only slightly tainted by boys who are juvenile criminals, while the repeated delinquent category is completely saturated with boys who have repeatedly and seriously violated the law. The differences found between the repeated delinquents and non-delinquents in this study in all likelihood can be referred in some way to differences in their behavior relevant to the legal norms of their society.

Chapter IV

ONE SET OF INTERVIEWS

Perhaps the best way to present the instruments which produced the family group and attitudinal data is to present a sample of interviews. From reading the sample, the reader will not only become more familiar with the questions boys and parents were asked but also with the kinds of answers respondents gave to them. So this chapter consists of the questions asked of and answers given by a repeated delinquent boy and his parents parallel with the answers given by his non-delinquent matched control and his parents. After presentation of the sample, some comments are made on material relevant to the various hypotheses advanced in Chapter II.

Of course, one set of cases proves nothing. These sample interviews are not offered as "typical." Both families involved have unique features, as does every other family in the study. In taking apart interviews in the process of content analysis, their uniqueness is inevitably lost, and the information obtained is to that extent removed from reality. But data extraction and abstraction are demanded by the process of scientific research. Undoubtedly, reading each of 635 interviews several times was necessary to understand the results of the data analysis; but data analysis was necessary to order the information in 635 interviews.

Not all the questions asked are included in the illustrative set. Several other interests aside from the one which guided this research contributed to the nature of the total instrument. Only those questions relevant to this study are presented. For example, questions which measured some personality dimensions among boys which are probably not linked to social status are not presented.

Each of the boys in this sample set was interviewed at his respective public junior high school. His interviewer called for him at a classroom prior to the start of an instruction period and led him to a private interviewing room. As they walked through the school corridors, the interviewer introduced himself to the youngster and explained what was to happen. Each boy was urged to ask

60

questions about the procedure if he wanted to. The interview began when youngster and interviewer were settled in the room. When the interview was finished, each interviewer recorded some thumbnail comments about his respondent.

BOYS' INTERVIEWS

Non-Delinquent	*Repeated Delinquent*
Boy's number 0880	Boy's number 0882

Boy's birth- day 1/13/44	Age at time of Interview 14	Boy's birth- day 5/30/44	Age at time of Interview 13
School Whittier Jr. High Grade 8		School Emerson Jr. High Grade 8	
I.Q. 109 Police Record: None		I.Q. 116 Police Record: 7 contacts	

4/15/55	Larc. from store
10/11/55	Larc. from bldg.
11/6/56	Auto theft and runaway
3/16/57	Destr. of property
4/15/57	Larc. from auto
8/16/57	Destr. of property
10/28/57	Runaway

Interviewer's Comments

This fella needs a good spanking. Cocksure in his attitude, neat in appearance and all, but feels he's past the stage of being treated like a youngster. Snickers at the job his father holds and appeared to enjoy having me take down his observations.

Blue jeans around his ankles; long, blond D.A. haircut. Really thought he was "neat"; implied that I was "square." Laughed at several questions. Tall, slim, good-looking. Dirty hands and nails and he kept picking them. He looked me "square in the eye" and laughed to tell me that I didn't impress him nor was he afraid of me.

---

1. Some boys like the town they live in and some boys don't. For all of us there are often things about a town a guy likes and other things he dislikes. Here is a card with several statements on it. Which *one* best fits how you feel about Flint?

	a very good place	
	more good than bad things	
X	good and bad things about equal	X
	more bad things than good	
	a very bad place	

Non-Delinquent   *Repeated Delinquent*

2. No matter how you feel about Flint, you might feel the same or different about the neighborhood where you live. Which one of those statements best fits how you feel about the neighborhood where you live?

> X   a very good place
>   more good than bad things
>   good and bad things about equal
>   more bad things than good   X
>   a very bad place

---

3. What *do* you like about your neighborhood?

The neighbors, and there are a lot of children my age.

There's a school around there to play basketball in. In the summer my boy-friend has places to play.

---

4. What *don't* you like about your neighborhood?

I don't like the people across the street.

A couple of the neighbors—they gos-sip.

---

6. Does your neighborhood have good places to play or hang around?

Yes, there's a school and a sand-lot.

I wouldn't say so.

---

7. Some neighborhoods in Flint have special places to play like parks or playgrounds or indoor places. Some have ice rinks, or swimming pools and places to play games or sports. Does your neighborhood have any of these?

> X   Yes
>   No   X

If YES, *ask:*   If NO, *ask:*

7a. Do you use any of them?   7c. Why not?

Yes.   (Interviewer failed to ask 7c.)

If YES, *ask:*

7b. Thinking of when you use them most, about how often would you say you used them?

Non-Delinquent	*Repeated Delinquent*
X several times a week once a week a few times a month once a month less than once a month	(Inap.: inappro- priate question)

8. How does your neighborhood compare to others in Flint on having swimming pools, parks, playgrounds, rinks, places for sports and things like that?

best in Flint X better than most average worse than most X worst in Flint	

9. Why, do you think, your neighborhood got a (better) (worse) (the same) deal on these things than (as) other neighborhoods?

It's not a slumming place. The kids seem to be clean-cut and everything. I never seem to get into trouble but I have been in trouble before.

Most neighborhoods have a community school around—we're about the same.

18. As you think ahead, what do you think are the things you will have to *make up your mind* about now or in the future?

About my education and whether to join the armed forces or not.

What I wanta do, what kind of job. If I'm going to finish school or not.

18a. Anything else?

No.

No.

19. You know, boys have all sorts of ideas about school. Some like going to school and some don't. How about you? How do you like school? Do you . . .

X like school a lot like school fairly well don't care one way or another X dislike school dislike school very much	

Non-Delinquent   *Repeated Delinquent*

20. What is the most important thing that makes you say you like (dislike) school?

(like)   (dislike)

Without an education, I don't   Some of the teachers.
feel I'd be anywhere.

---

21. Do you want to quit school when you're 16?

	Yes	
X	No	X

21c. Why not?

I need an education to make   I want to finish high school.
something of myself.

21d. Do you think you will quit school when you're 16?

	Yes	
X	No	X

---

22. If you did quit school, do you think your parents would . . .

    X   try to make you go on in school
             feel disappointed, but do nothing   X
             leave it up to you
             Be glad when you quit

---

23. What do you think it means to be a "success?"

Oh, to have friends . . . setting   Have everything you want.
a goal and reaching it, then
setting another goal.

---

24. How much would you say you've thought about what job you'll have when you're older—a great deal, some, a little, or what?

    X   a great deal
             some
             a little   X
             no thoughts about it

Non-Delinquent	*Repeated Delinquent*

25. What job would you like to have when you take a job?

Law or medicine	Right now in a grocery store. Later on I'd like to have my own business.

If he has some job in mind, ask:

25a. What kind of job would that be?

Well, for law, I'd be a lawyer, then I think I'd go on in politics. As a doctor, I'd be a chiropractor.	I'd like to have a restaurant or a grocery.

26. How sure are you about wanting that job? Very sure? Pretty sure? Not so sure? Or what?

	very sure	
X	pretty sure	X
	not so sure	

27. What do you suppose is the real reason you want that job?

I want to be something and a doctor or a lawyer seems to be a respectable person.	I don't know.

If had some job in mind, continue to ask:

28. What do you think are your chances of getting that job?

	very good	X
X	fair	
	even, 50-50	
	poor	
	very bad	

29. What makes (would make) it *easy* to get that kind of job?

Good marks—and *wanting* to do it, not being forced to do it.	I know the people that own it.

30. What makes (would make) it *hard* to get that kind of job?

Oh—the time it would require. A guy might lose interest.	If jobs are all filled up and they don't need help.

Non-Delinquent   *Repeated Delinquent*

ASK EVERYONE

31. Some people say that every boy in the United States has an equal chance
    to get the job he wants. Other people say that some boys have a better
    chance to get the jobs they want. How do you feel about that?   Do you
    feel that every boy in this country has as good a chance as every other
    boy to get the job he wants?

    Yes—you can do what you want   Yes—Because there's plenty of jobs
    to be.   and everyone's got a chance.

31a. How about you?   Do you have a better, worse, or equal chance?

                              better chance
              X   equal chance   X
                              worse chance

32. What will you probably do when you get out of high school?

    Go on to college.   Get a job. (Probe) Working in a
                                           grocery store or something.

32a. What will you probably do after that?

    Oh—go into business for myself,   Save and buy my own business.
    probably medicine.

    I: How old will you be then?

    I guess about 27 or 30.   21 years old.

32b. What will you probably do next?

    Get married, I guess, when I'm   Build a chain of stores.
    about 27. Raise children, try
    to give my wife and children a
    good life.

32c. And then?

    I'd stress education to my   That's all.
    children.

    (Continue until R no longer
    projects a change.)

| | *Non-Delinquent* | *Repeated Delinquent* |

33. What does your father do for a living?

He works in the factory, at   He works in a factory.
Buick.

If not clear, *ask:*

33a. What exactly does he do?

Well, I don't know.   Working on utility—keeping furnaces
                                      going and stuff.

---

34. Do you think he would rather do something else instead of what he's
doing?

	yes, definitely	X
X	yes, perhaps	
	undecided (refers to father's decision, not boy's)	
	no, probably	
	no, definitely	

If YES, *ask:*

34a. What would he rather do?

He'd rather be independent—his   He wants a business of his own.
own business.

---

35. How would you like your father's job if you had it?

	like it very much	
	like it more than dislike it	
	don't care one way or another	X
	dislike it more than like it	
X	dislike it very much	

---

36. Now thinking of other men you know, like a brother who is working, or
a friend's father, or some men in your neighborhood. . . . How do you
think *most* of them feel about their jobs?

X	like it very much	
	like it more than dislike it	
	don't care one way or another	
	dislike it more than like it	X
	dislike it very much	

Non-Delinquent   *Repeated Delinquent*

37. Do any of those people that you thought of have jobs you'd like to have?

       X   Yes
                      No   X

If YES, *ask:*

37a. What jobs do they have that you'd like?

My brother-in-law is studying   (Inap.)
law. And my father's friend is
a chiropractor.

---

38. When you're grown up who do you want to be like?

Like my next-door neighbor—his   Nobody in particular.
name is Dean L. _____

If R mentions anybody, ask:

38a. Why do you want to be like him (her) (them)?

He seems to be a real nice guy.   (Inap.)
He has a nice job— K. _____
Textile Products—he's personnel
manager. And he's nice to his
little boy.

---

40. Who would you rather be like as a person . . . .

       X   Pat Boone, or
                    Elvis Presley   X

---

41. Sometimes boys do things they shouldn't do, but these things aren't very serious, just sort of wild. Sometimes they do things that are more serious. I'm going to read to you some things a boy your age might do. Can you tell me whether (persons above in Q. 38) would think it was: OK, wild but not serious, getting serious, very serious, or what?

                           (He laughed at all these questions and
                           his answers were all sarcastic.)

If boy has named *no* model in Q. 38, *ask:*

41a. Can you tell me whether . . . (Boone or Presley) . . . would think it was: OK, wild but not serious, getting serious, very serious, or what?

Non-Delinquent   *Repeated Delinquent*

a. First, breaking into the school cafeteria at night with some friends and eating a pie.

                OK
                wild but not serious   X
                getting serious
    X   very serious
                don't know

b. Next, breaking into school at night with some friends and throwing over wastebaskets and desks.

                OK
                wild but not serious
                getting serious
    X   very serious   X
                don't know

c. And, breaking into school at night with some friends and breaking up desks and tables and smearing paint on the walls.

                OK
                wild but not serious
                getting serious
    X   very serious   X
                don't know

---

42. Have you ever been in trouble with the police?

No   Yes

If YES, *ask:*

42a. What about?

(Inap.)   B and E (Break and enter), and a stolen car.

42b. How did you feel?

(Inap.)   Bad.

---

43. If a boy had been in trouble with the police do you think this would make any difference to what he might want or be able to do in the future?

It might and it might not. A lot of boys get into trouble with the police and the police help them out and understand their fault and they become good people.

Yes, because it will influence the person you're going to work for.

Non-Delinquent   *Repeated Delinquent*

If R has a father, ask:

44. When you think of how you should do things or what you ought to do . . .
    do you feel that you and your father always agree, usually, sometimes,
    seldom, never, or what?

	always	(He laughed here again.)
X	usually	
	sometimes	X
	seldom	
	never	

If R has a mother, ask:

45. When you think of how you should do things or what you ought to do . . .
    do you feel that you and your mother always agree, usually, sometimes,
    seldom, never, or what?

	always	
X	usually	
	sometimes	X
	seldom	
	never	

---

48. If you had some personal problem you wanted to talk about with some-
    one, who do you feel you could talk with? Who would you most likely
    go to?

My older sister (I: How old   Between my mother and father. . . .
is she?) She's 21.   I never talk to them about my prob-
                                      lems.

---

49. What have you done that made your *parents* angry, upset, or disappointed
    in you?

Arguing with my younger sister   Fight with my brother at home.
—she's older than I (she's 16)
but younger than my 21-year-
old sister.

49a. When did that happen?

Every day—nothing serious   All the time.

---

50. What have you done that your parents have liked most, things they were
    glad you did?

I don't smoke. I get good   I bring home things we made—Metal
grades in school, and I never   Shop.
got in serious trouble.

Non-Delinquent	*Repeated Delinquent*

50a. When did that happen?

I get good grades regularly.   Oh . . . Every year.

---

51. If you do something wrong at home, how do you get punished?

My father usually talks to me   I don't usually get punished.
and tells me why I shouldn't do
it. I never receive lickings or
anything. My parents feel I'm
old enough to understand.

---

52. About how often do you get punished for something?

Twice a year.   I hardly ever do anything because
                 I'm hardly ever home.

---

53. Thinking of the things you have got punished for, do you get punished
every time you do them, usually, occasionally, or what?

	punished every time; consistent	
	punished every time if caught	
X	punished most of the time	
	punished only occasionally	X

---

54. Do you think the punishment you usually get is too tough, about fair, or
too easy?

	too tough, too hard	
X	fair	
	too easy	X

If R has a father, ask:

55. What sort of things do you usually do with your father?

Oh we do a lot of work together.   I don't do nothin' with him.
(Probe) Yardwork. We go to
fights. We play cards and games.

If R has a mother, ask:

56. What sort of things do you usually do with your mother?

I go to the movies—with my   Nothin'.
mother and father. Sometimes
I might help her work around
the house.

Non-Delinquent   *Repeated Delinquent*

62. Now I have one last question. All in all how do you feel about your life
    ahead?

X	real good	
	fairly good	X
	so-so; don't care	
	not so good	
	real bad	

Several weeks after the interviews were taken, all the boys in
the sample in each school were assembled in school auditoriums
where an interviewer explained that the Flint Youth Study now wanted
them to respond to a paper-and-pencil questionnaire. It was stressed
that the questionnaire was not a school test. The interviewer read
each question aloud as the boys proceeded through the questionnaire.

Again, only questionnaire items relevant to this study are presented.

Boys' Questionnaire

Non-Delinquent

Boy's number ___0880___

1. Here is a list. Opposite each item put a check (√) under LIKE if you
   like it, under DISLIKE if you do not like it, and under DON'T CARE if
   you feel you do not care one way or another.

2. Now use the same list again. Put a check for each one in the second
   column, on the right, for the choice that you think YOUR FATHER WOULD
   MAKE FOR HIMSELF. If you don't have a father, make the choices you
   think your uncle or grandfather or some other man would make if a man
   like that lives in your home. If no man lives in your home, check the
   box below and *wait* to go on to the next question.

For Yourself			For Your Father			
Like	Don't Care	Dis-like	LIKE	DON'T CARE	DIS-LIKE	
___	___	√	√	___	___	a. repairing a clock
√	___	___	___	___	√	b. making a speech
√	___	___	√	___	___	c. reading a book
√	___	___	√	___	___	d. playing baseball
___	___	√	___	___	√	e. living in the country
√	___	___	___	___	√	f. driving a car
√	___	___	√	___	___	g. watching a boxing match

Interview with a boy.

Wieland

Repeated Delinquent

| | | For Yourself | | | For Your Father | |
	Like	Don't Care	Dis-like	LIKE	DON'T CARE	DIS-LIKE
a. repairing a clock		✓			✓	
b. making a speech		✓				✓
c. reading a book	✓			✓		
d. playing baseball	✓				✓	
e. living in the country	✓			✓		
f. driving a car	✓				✓	
g. watching a boxing match		✓		✓		

Non-Delinquent

For Yourself			For Your Father			
Like	Don't Care	Dis-like	LIKE	DON'T CARE	DIS-LIKE	
√			√			h. listening to a symphony concert
√			√			i. playing chess
		√	√			j. solving a mechanical puzzle
√			√			k. arithmetic
√			√			l. English
√			√			m. music
√			√			n. gym
√			√			o. history

Non-Delinquent   *Repeated Delinquent*

4. In every family there is a certain amount of disagreement about how things should be done. Usually there is some talk about it, and then a decision is made. Sometimes the father in the family has more to say in what the decision is than the mother does, and sometimes the mother has more to say. Here is a list of things your family might have decided about sometime or might have to decide about in the future. After each one, you check how often you think your mother or your father would have the final say in the decision about it, in your family.

1. Who would have the final say if your father and mother disagreed about *where to go for a vacation?*
   - ____ mother always ____
   - ____ mother usually, father sometimes ____
   - √ mother and father, 50-50   √
   - ____ father usually, mother sometimes ____
   - ____ father always ____

2. Who would have the final say if your father and mother disagreed about *which doctor to call when someone was sick?*
   - ____ mother always ____
   - ____ mother usually, father sometimes   √
   - √ mother and father, 50-50 ____
   - ____ father usually, mother sometimes ____
   - ____ father always ____

Repeated Delinquent

	For Yourself			For Your Father		
	Like	Don't Care	Dis-like	LIKE	DON'T CARE	DIS-LIKE
h. listening to a symphony concert		✓				✓
i. playing chess		✓				✓
j. solving a mechanical puzzle		✓				✓
k. arithmetic		✓		✓		
l. English	✓				✓	
m. music			✓		✓	
n. gym	✓				✓	
o. history		✓			✓	

Non-Delinquent   *Repeated Delinquent*

3. Who would have the final say if your father and mother disagreed about *your mother taking a job or a different job?*

____	mother always	_____
____	mother usually, father sometimes	_____
✓	mother and father, 50-50	_____
____	father usually, mother sometimes	_____
____	father always	✓

4. Who would have the final say if your father and mother disagreed about *what car to buy?*

____	mother always	_____
____	mother usually, father sometimes	_____
✓	mother and father, 50-50	✓
____	father usually, mother sometimes	_____
____	father always	_____

5. Who would have the final say if your father and mother disagreed about *how much money to spend on food for the family?*

____	mother always	_____
____	mother usually, father sometimes	_____
✓	mother and father, 50-50	✓
____	father usually, mother sometimes	_____
____	father always	_____

Non-Delinquent   *Repeated Delinquent*

6. Who would have the final say if your father and mother disagreed about *giving you permission to do something?*

    ____   mother always   ____
    ____   mother usually, father sometimes   ____
    √   mother and father, 50-50   ____
    ____   father usually, mother sometimes   √
    ____   father always   ____

7. Who would have the final say if your father and mother disagreed about *which new house or apartment to move to?*

    ____   mother always   ____
    ____   mother usually, father sometimes   ____
    √   mother and father, 50-50   √
    ____   father usually, mother sometimes   ____
    ____   father always   ____

8. Who would have the final say if your father and mother disagreed about *buying life insurance?*

    ____   mother always   ____
    ____   mother usually, father sometimes   ____
    √   mother and father, 50-50   √
    ____   father usually, mother sometimes   ____
    ____   father always   ____

9. Who would have the final say if your mother and father disagreed about *your father changing his job?*

    ____   mother always   ____
    ____   mother usually, father sometimes   ____
    √   mother and father, 50-50   ____
    ____   father usually, mother sometimes   √
    ____   father always   ____

17. Here are some reasons boys give for going all the way through high school. Put a "1" opposite the *one* you think would be the *one most important reason for you.* Put a "2" opposite the *second most important one for you.* Do not write more than one "1" or more than one "2."

    ___ a. you meet people and make friends   ___
    ___ b. you need a high school diploma to   1
          get the job you want
    2 c. you need a high school diploma
          to go to college   ___
    ___ d. you keep busy and out of trouble,   2
          because high school gives you
          something to do

Non-Delinquent   *Repeated Delinquent*

<u>1</u> e. you learn to behave right   ___
___ f. you have fun learning things in
high school   ___

---

18. How much interest do you feel your teachers have taken in your future? (check one).

√	a great deal	___
___	some	√
___	very little	___
___	none	___

---

19. Here is a list of jobs. Please rate each job on how good you think it is generally. You either may or may not want any of the jobs yourself, but you can still rate it on how good a job you think it is. For example, you might not want to be a farmer but you might think of it as a pretty good job anyway. Please put a check in the column which you think best describes each job.

Excellent	Good	So-So	Poor		Excellent	Good	So-So	Poor
___	√	___	___	a. office manager	___	√	___	___
___	___	___	√	b. waiter	___	___	___	√
___	√	___	___	c. advertising exec.	___	___	√	___
___	√	___	___	d. bookkeeper	___	___	___	√
___	√	___	___	e. TV repairman	___	___	√	___
√	___	___	___	f. judge	___	___	√	___
___	___	___	√	g. assembly line worker	___	___	___	√
___	___	√	___	h. real estate salesman	___	___	√	___
√	___	___	___	i. chemical engineer	___	___	√	___
___	___	√	___	j. factory manager	___	√	___	___

Non-Delinquent						Repeated Delinquent			
Excel-lent	Good	So-So	Poor			Excel-lent	Good	So-So	Poor
		√		k. store clerk			√		
			√	l. spot welder				√	

20. Lastly, read these statements one by one. After you have read one, make up your mind whether you agree or disagree. Then whether you are sure or just think so. Then put a check (√) in the column you have chosen.

> When I become an adult I'd like to be the kind of person my father is.
>
> √   Sure I agree   ___
> ___   Think I agree   √
> ___   Think I disagree   ___
> ___   Sure I disagree   ___

Parents were all interviewed at home, on separate days. The interview with the father of the non-delinquent was not as private as the others because his 16-year-old daughter seemed to have reasons for passing through the living room frequently. The interviewers felt all the parents were frank and none seemed to resist being interviewed. The father of the repeated delinquent seemed angry and upset at the time, and for good reason.

Mothers' Interviews

Non-Delinquent	Repeated Delinquent

Interviewer's Comments

The home is situated in one of the better Flint sections—a brand new above-middle-class home. It is very well furnished—above average type of furnishings. Extremely well-kept and apparently a thing of pride to its owner.

The respondent is a handsome woman with an extremely pleasant personality. She answered all the questions in a straightforward positive manner. As a

She is a nice and lovely lady. She seems unhappy, but thinks a lot of her children. Seems honest and frank.

The house is in a poor neighborhood. Her furniture is old but clean and neat.

She answered all the questions with the best of her knowledge.

Non-Delinquent   *Repeated Delinquent*

Interviewer's Comments (Cont'd)

matter of fact, she seemed to have
positive feelings about everything I
questioned her about. She was very
interested in this research program,
was sure it was worthwhile, and expressed a great deal of interest in
its results.

---

1. First of all, we're interested in getting a picture of your family. Will
   you tell me who lives here at home with you? How old is he (she)?

   A_____, my husband—49.   My husband, he's 46, J_____.
   My daughter, G_____, she's   And my middle son, R_____, 15,
   16. And Phil, he's 14.   and my youngest son, Jimmy, you
                                    know, 14.

1a. Do you have any children who live away from home now?

   X   Yes   X
                  No

(IF YES)

1a. Who might that be? How old is he (she)?

   I have a married daughter   There's my oldest son, J _____, Jr.,
   21 years old, J_____.   in the air force, he's 18, and my
                                   daughter, S_____, who's away in
                                   school.

---

15. Do you do any part-time or full-time work for pay?

                  none   X
                  part-time
   X   full-time

IF R WORKS:

18. Does your work have any effect on your family life?

   X   Yes   (Inap.)
                  No

| *Non-Delinquent* | *Repeated Delinquent* |

(IF YES)

18a. In what way?

| You can't be a full-time house-wife and mother—you can't do justice to your home. On the other hand, it helps provide many things we couldn't otherwise have. | |

19. How do you think a woman's life is changed by having children?

| It gives her a lot more responsibility and it makes her more tolerant and understanding. It gives her a lot of extra work. | You're busier, you have more worries. And it is a pleasure to raise your own children. . . . It's complicated. And you have something to look forward in the future. |

20. In bringing up children, what do you try to do—what are your general aims?

| To bring my children up to be honest, conscientious, and sincere and to do the best they can whatever they try to do. | I want them to go to church; I want them to go to school, and to be good citizens. |

20a. What other things do you try to do?

| I try to teach them to respect others, to be fair with all. | I want them to work around the house and have their recreation too . . . to love them. |

20b. Which of these things do you regard as the most important?

| To be honest and sincere. | An education. |

20c. Which would you say is the next most important?

| To do the best they can in anything they do. | Church. |

21. What ideas and hopes have you had about your son's future?

| I have hoped he would pick a fine profession for himself. He would be a success, and be honest and *upright*—most of all. | He wants to be a hairdresser, so I think I will like it too. |

Non-Delinquent   *Repeated Delinquent*

22. When are you and _____ (son) typically home at the same time?

In the evenings when he stays   Every evening. . . .
home . . . Saturdays and Sundays,
all day.

(If not mentioned)

22a. How about on weekends?

                                   And every weekend.

---

23. At times when you're both home, what things might you and your son be
doing together, if anything?

He always helps me around the   Watching TV. . . . I help him in his
house very much. We watch   homework. . . . We wash dishes and
television together. We talk to   play cards.
each other, eat together.

---

24. What sorts of things does _____ (son) bring up to talk about with you?

He'll discuss things that have   About the teachers, friends, his dis-
gone on in school—about his   likes and likes, what he wants to be
friends, his plans. We discuss   when he grows up. And he tells me
how the different professions   the shows he goes and sees.
would be. He complains about
what he hasn't got or had to do.
He asks for things he would like.

---

26. What would you most like to change, if anything, about _____ (son) if
you could, about his ability or personality or behavior or looks or anything?

To be more tolerant. (I: What   I would like to change his funny be-
do you mean?) I'd like him to   havior—his laughing about everything.
change in his spending. He's   I wish he would like to do school-
too careless and carefree with   work.
money. I'd like him to apply
himself a little more in school.
He's at a smarty age. I'd like
him to be more quiet and re-
served.

---

28. How much schooling do you think _____ (son) will really need for
what he's likely to do when he's an adult?

                    (1) grade school
                    (2) high school   X
          X   (3) college
                    (4) more than college

Non-Delinquent   *Repeated Delinquent*

29. How much schooling do you expect your son will have?

Through college   High school

---

30. Here are some reasons people give us for boys going through high school.
     (HAND R CARD 11)   With your own son in mind, which of these reasons
     do you think is most important?   (Put a "1" next to 1st choice.)

___	(1) to meet people and make friends	___
2	(2) to get a good job	1
1	(3) to get into college	___
___	(4) to keep busy and out of trouble	2
___	(5) to learn how to behave right	___
___	(6) to have fun	___

---

31. If your son decided to quit school when he reached the age of 17, would
     you: (HAND R CARD 12)

     X   (1)   insist he go on in school
         (2)   try to keep him interested in school   X
         (3)   feel disappointed but do nothing
         (4)   be glad he quit

---

32. What kind of job would you like him to have as an adult?

I would like him to have a pro-   I would like the job he wants. I
fession like engineering—a pro-   think it's a useful job.
fession he could get a job with
any place he goes. He will
have to decide for himself,
though.

---

33. What do you think his chances are of getting that kind of job?

             (1)   very good
             (2)   fair
     X   (3)   50-50, even   X
             (4)   poor
             (5)   very bad

WHERE A FATHER IS IN THE HOME

34. How would you feel about your son taking a job like your husband's?
     (HAND R CARD 13)

             (1)   like it very much
             (2)   like it more than dislike it
             (3)   don't care one way or another   X
     X   (4)   dislike it more than like it
             (5)   dislike it very much

Non-Delinquent   *Repeated Delinquent*

35. Some people say that every boy in the United States has an equal chance of getting the job he wants. Other people say that some boys have a better chance than others to get the job they want. Do you think all boys have an equal chance of getting the jobs they want?

	Yes	
X	No	X

35a. Why do you say that?

Sometimes they are not fit for the job they want—it may not be available at the time. They don't make an effort to get the job they want, sometimes.

They have an equal chance, if they get help and they help themselves.

35b. How about your own son? Do you think he will find it *somewhat easier, about equal,* or *somewhat harder* than most other boys to get the job he may want?

	somewhat easier	
	equal	X
X	somewhat harder	

36. Now I'd like to talk with you a bit about children growing up, and the things that happen. What sorts of things has _____ (son) done that have made you angry, upset, or disappointed in him?

Phil is a boy with a good disposition. He is quite obedient. At this stage he's too talkative; that's about all.

A year ago he swiped things in the store and he got picked up twice.

37. Thinking of the times when _____ (son) has misbehaved in the past one or two years, what have you usually done about it?

I have disciplined him and explained why. I usually take his privileges away.

I punished him . . . and talked things over.

39. Sometimes boys do things they shouldn't do, but these things aren't very serious, just sort of wild. Sometimes they do things that are more serious. I'm going to read to you some things a boy your son's age might do. Will you tell me whether you think it was (HAND R CARD 15). . . OK? wild but not serious? getting serious? or very serious?

Here's the first one . . .   Card 15

Non-Delinquent   *Repeated Delinquent*

39a. Stealing a car, joy-riding in it, and abandoning it.

	(1)	OK	
	(2)	wild but not serious	
	(3)	getting serious	
X	(4)	very serious	X
	(5)	don't know	

39b. Breaking into the school cafeteria at night with some friends and eating a pie.

	(1)	OK	
	(2)	wild but not serious	
	(3)	getting serious	
X	(4)	very serious	X
	(5)	don't know	

39c. Next, breaking into school at night with some friends and throwing over wastebaskets and desks.

	(1)	OK	
	(2)	wild but not serious	
	(3)	getting serious	
X	(4)	very serious	X
	(5)	don't know	

39d. And, breaking into school at night with some friends and breaking up desks and tables and smearing paint on the walls.

	(1)	OK	
	(2)	wild but not serious	
	(3)	getting serious	
X	(4)	very serious	X
	(5)	don't know	

40. When _____ (son) does something he's **not** supposed to do, something you don't approve of, which of these things are you most likely to do? (HAND R CARD 16) (Put a "1" in the proper space below.)

____	(1)	Spank him or hit him	
____	(2)	Threaten to spank him or hit him	____
1	(3)	Deprive him of something he likes, like a treat or a privilege	1
____	(4)	Scold him, yell at him	
2	(5)	Tell him or show him you are disappointed in him	2
____	(6)	Point out how he should behave, talk it over	____
____	(7)	Show no feeling about it	____
____	(8)	Just wait until he does what you want, then praise him	____

Non-Delinquent   *Repeated Delinquent*

41. What sorts of things has _____ (son) done that you have liked very much, things you were glad he did?

When he's considerate, honest. He's good most of the time. (I: For example?) No special time.	Coming straight home from school, and going steadily to school. And he stayed away from trouble.

46. Do you as a parent try to influence your son in his choice of friends?

X	Yes	
	No	X

(IF YES)

46a. In what ways?

I tell him to pick boys who are brought up the same way Phil has been . . . honest boys, boys with clean habits, not rowdy boys.	(Inap.)

47. How much influence would you say you have in your son's selection of friends? (HAND R CARD 19)

X	(1)	a great deal	X
	(2)	some	
	(3)	very little	
	(4)	almost none	

48. Do you think it makes a difference whether or not your son has any friends who have ever been picked up by the police?

X	Yes	X
	No	

(IF YES)

48a. In what ways?

It showed they have something in common and were therefore attracted to each other. It would mean Phil was the same way as the boy with the police record. I wouldn't want him to be a bad influence on Phil.	I would rather he goes around with the boys that do not have a record. It would be bad policy for him.

Non-Delinquent   *Repeated Delinquent*

49. No boy grows up without getting into trouble of one sort or another.
     That's part of growing up.   What do you think is the most serious trou-
     ble _____ (son) has gotten into so far?   What happened?

Before we moved here, there   A year ago and another time just
was a man who had his brief-   before Christmas '57, he got in
case stolen. My son and a boy   trouble swiping things from a store
were suspected of stealing the   around here.
briefcase. The detectives
proved it wasn't Phil, it was
the other boy.

49a. Why do you think it happened?

A group of boys were standing   Oh, just to show off.
around talking and in the com-
pany of the boy who was later
suspected. The man who lost
the case asked Phil to help him
find out who had stolen it.

49b. What did you do?

We talked to Phil and asked   I punished him, and deprived him of
him to be honest and truthful;   things he liked.
asked him if he was telling
the truth and to cooperate with
the man.

49f. How do you think it turned out?

Very well, because Phil realized   Good.   Jimmy promised not to do it
it didn't pay to be in the com-   again.
pany of such boys. After that
Phil refused to associate with
those boys by himself.

49g. Do you expect problems of this sort and others will keep coming
      up?

                              Yes   X
             X   No

49h. What makes you guess they will (won't)?

Phil's friends all seem to be   I am afraid he will do it again.
boys that aren't that kind and   He is a nervous type boy.
neither is Phil.

Non-Delinquent   *Repeated Delinquent*

51. What do you think a parent like yourself should do if your boy stole a car, went joy-riding in it, and abandoned it?

I would discipline my boy, I   Punish him and talk reason to him.
would see that he made it good
and it wouldn't happen again.

---

52. What do you think the police should do with a boy they've picked up for stealing a car, joy-riding in it, and abandoning it?

I don't know . . . I haven't the   They should punish them.
slightest idea of what they would
do. (I: What do you think?) . . .
I still don't know.

---

53. Most parents disagree sometimes about how the children should be handled. About how often would you say that you and your husband disagree about this? (HAND R CARD 20)

X	(1) quite often	X
	(2) sometimes	
	(3) hardly ever	
	(4) never	

53a. What are the things you don't agree on?
(BE SURE TO GET WHO TAKES WHICH POSITION)

I am more lenient. We don't   I couldn't say.
agree on staying out late—he
is more strict about that. I
tell them to do something
once or twice. He keeps
after them and doesn't think
they should be told twice.

53b. What other things might you disagree on?

I keep after them; if they don't   (Inap.)
do it I'll do it myself.

I will give in to their food likes.
He feels they should eat what's
served. I try to satisfy their
likes or dislikes more.

---

54. Husbands and wives may often disagree about things. When you and your husband disagree about something, who has the final say in the decision?

Non-Delinquent   *Repeated Delinquent*

54a.   For example, if you and your husband disagreed about where to go for a vacation, who would have the final say? (HAND R CARD 21)

           (1)   wife always
           (2)   wife usually, husband sometimes
   X   (3)   wife and husband about the same   X
           (4)   husband usually, wife sometimes
           (5)   husband always

54b.   Suppose you disagreed about which doctor to call when someone was ill, who would have the final say?

   X   (1)   wife always
           (2)   wife usually, husband sometimes
           (3)   wife and husband about the same   X
           (4)   husband usually, wife sometimes
           (5)   husband always

54c.   . . . about your taking a job or a different job?

           (1)   wife always
           (2)   wife usually, husband sometimes
           (3)   wife and husband about the same
           (4)   husband usually, wife sometimes
   X   (5)   husband always   X

54d.   . . . about which car to buy?

           (1)   wife always
           (2)   wife usually, husband sometimes
           (3)   wife and husband about the same   X
           (4)   husband usually, wife sometimes
   X   (5)   husband always

54e.   . . . about how much money to spend on food for the family?

           (1)   wife always   X
           (2)   wife usually, husband sometimes
   X   (3)   wife and husband about the same
           (4)   husband usually, wife sometimes
           (5)   husband always

54f.   . . . about giving your son permission to do something?

           (1)   wife always
           (2)   wife usually, husband sometimes
   X   (3)   wife and husband about the same
           (4)   husband usually, wife sometimes   X
           (5)   husband always

Non-Delinquent   *Repeated Delinquent*

54g. . . . about which new house or apartment to move to?

             (1) wife always
   X (2) wife usually, husband sometimes
             (3) wife and husband about the same X
             (4) husband usually, wife sometimes
             (5) husband always

54h. . . . about buying life insurance?

             (1) wife always
             (2) wife usually, husband sometimes
             (3) wife and husband about the same X
             (4) husband usually, wife sometimes
   X (5) husband always

54i. . . . about your husband changing his job?

             (1) wife always   X
             (2) wife usually, husband sometimes
             (3) wife and husband about the same
             (4) husband usually, wife sometimes
   X (5) husband always

55. When you think of how your son should do things or what he ought to do
. . . do you feel that you and he agree?   (HAND R CARD 22)

             (1) always
             (2) usually   X
   X (3) sometimes
             (4) seldom
             (5) never

Now in order to compare your answers with other people's, we need to know
something about where you were born and things like that.   So I'm going to
finish this interview with some questions about you.

56. Where were you born?   (If U.S. get city and state; if elsewhere, get
country.)

  C_____, Illinois   B_____, Arkansas

57. What is your birthdate?

  April 2, 1916   May 6, 1919

58. What was the highest grade of school you completed?

  I completed high school.   Seven years.

Non-Delinquent   *Repeated Delinquent*

59. Did you grow up on a farm, or in a small town, or city, or what?

In a large city.   In a rural home, in Arkansas.

Fathers' Interviews

Non-Delinquent   *Repeated Delinquent*

Interviewer's Comments

Neighborhood upper middle-class, well-kept section of the city. Neat and clean inside, inexpensively but tastefully furnished. R neatly groomed suit and tie. R is short (5'6") and medium build, slightly balding on top of head and graying hair. Dark complexion and wore glasses. R has pronounced accent and poor grammar. R spoke haltingly at first and said little. He became more fluent and began to answer questions before I had finished asking them. R seemed to answer the questions where the card responses were used before he or I had a chance to read all the possible responses.

R seems to be a very strict disciplinarian and has faith that his children are always honest with him and tell him their problems. From talking with R after the interview, I receive the impression that he is on very friendly terms with his neighbors.

Tall fellow, quite heavy (6'—200 lbs.) wears glasses. Wore a cap all the time.

First two fingers missing from right hand.

Not well-spoken but definitely amiable. Proud of his family, but worried about his son. (The boy had stolen a car a few hours before the interview.) Evidenced distinct signs of lung congestion, blames shop (Buick).

---

2. (Now) I'd like to get your opinions about a number of things. First, some people like the town they live in and some people don't. For all of us there are often things about a town one likes and other things one dislikes. Here is a card with several statements on it. Which **one** best fits how you feel about Flint?

       X   (1)   a very good place
             (2)   more good than bad things
             (3)   good and bad things about equal
             (4)   more bad things than good   X
             (5)   a very bad place

Non-Delinquent   *Repeated Delinquent*

3. No matter how you feel about Flint, you might feel the same or different about the neighborhood where you live. Which one of these statements best fits how you feel about the neighborhood where you live?

    X (1) a very good place   X
       (2) more good than bad things
       (3) good and bad things about equal
       (4) more bad things than good
       (5) a very bad place

15c. What kind of work do you do? (IF NOT CLEAR) What exactly do you do?

A sheet metal worker—a tin- A gas furnace man—heat treatment
smith.   at Buick.

15d. Where do you work?

Buick   Buick

---

16. If you had a chance to get another job, would you take it?

    X   Yes
          No   X

IF YES, ASK:

16a. What kind of job would that be?

Better than I've got.   (Inap.)

16c. What do you think your chances are of getting that kind of job? (HAND R CARD 10)

        (1) very good   (Inap.)
        (2) fair
    X   (3) even, 50-50
        (4) poor
        (5) very bad

16d. Have you tried to get a job like that?

    X   Yes   (Inap.)
          No

Non-Delinquent   *Repeated Delinquent*

IF YES, ASK:

16e. What happened?

I got it. I used to be a press-   (Inap.)
man, in the shop.

(SEE ANSWER TO Q. 16)

17. You said you would (not) take another job if you got the chance. What
    do you suppose is the real reason why you've stayed with the job you
    have?

    (Inap.)   I've got seniority.

---

18. Does your work have any effect on your family life?

                          Yes   X
              X   No

---

19. How do you think a man's life is changed by having children?

    There is a lot of noise (from   It changes 100 per cent. You got
    the kids).   more responsibilities.

    19a. What other things can you think of?

    Financially, when you are not   You have more freedom without chil-
    able to give your kids what they   dren.
    need.

---

20. In bringing up children, what do you try to do—what are your general
    aims?

    Oh . . . give them advice, teach   Teach them right from wrong—give
    them discipline, not to talk back   them an education.
    to elders. Just like I was taught.

    20a. What other things do you try to do?

    I try to talk to them, tell them   Well . . . keep them happy, I guess
    to go on to college.   . . . and out of trouble.

    20b. Which of these things do you regard as the most important?

    Not to follow in my footsteps.   Right and wrong . . . and education.

Non-Delinquent   *Repeated Delinquent*

20c. Which would you say is the next most important?

To behave theirself and be   . . . education.
honest.

---

21. What ideas and hopes have you had about your son's future?

He's gonna go to college. (R   I'd like to see him be a barber.
seemed to want the boy to get
through college and then decide
what he wants to do; R was
quite emphatic about not trying
to choose a job for son.)

---

24. What sorts of things does _____ (son) bring up to talk about with you?

His schooling   I wouldn't want to put it on paper.

---

26. What would you most like to change, if anything, about _____ (son) if
you could, about his ability or personality or behavior or looks or anything?

Nothing—I couldn't ask for more   His personality, I guess.
than he already is . . . Nothing . . .
he knows the difference between
right and wrong.

---

28. How much schooling do you think _____ (son) will really need for
what he's likely to do when he's an adult?

              (1) grade school   X
              (2) high school
              (3) college
    X   (4) more than college

---

29. How much schooling do you expect your son will have?

Through college   Grade school

30. Here are some reasons people give us for boys going through high school.
(HAND R CARD 11). With your own son in mind, which of these reasons
do you think is most important? (Put a "1" next to 1st choice.) Which
would you say is the next most important? (Put a "2" next to second
choice.)

    ____ (1) to meet people and make friends ____
    ____ (2) to get a good job   ____

Non-Delinquent			*Repeated Delinquent*
_1_	(3)	to get into college	_1_
_2_	(4)	to keep busy and out of trouble	_2_
___	(5)	to learn how to behave right	___
___	(6)	to have fun	___

---

31. If your son decided to quit school when he reached the age of 16, would you: (HAND R CARD 12)

      X   (1)   insist he go on in school
           (2)   try to keep him interested in school
           (3)   feel disappointed but do nothing   X
           (4)   be glad he quit

---

32. What kind of job would you like him to have as an adult?

That's up to himself. Just so he goes to college.   It wouldn't make much difference, it depends on him.

---

33. What do you think his chances are of getting that kind of job? (HAND R CARD 10)

      X   (1)   very good   'X
               (2)   fair
               (3)   50-50, even
               (4)   poor
               (5)   very bad

---

34. How would you feel about your son taking a job like yours? (HAND R CARD 13)

             (1)   like it very much   X
             (2)   like it more than dislike it
             (3)   don't care one way or another
      X   (4)   dislike it more than like it
             (5)   dislike it very much

---

35. Some people say that every boy in the United States has an equal chance of getting the job he wants. Other people say that some boys have a better chance than others to get the job they want. Do you think all boys have an equal chance of getting the jobs they want?

      X   Yes
                   No   X

35a. Why do you say that?

If they take advantage of it, they can always get what they want. They can work their way through college.   It's a family affair . . . some help, some don't care.

Non-Delinquent   *Repeated Delinquent*

35b. How about your own son? Do you think he will find it *somewhat easier, about equal,* or *somewhat harder* than most other boys to get the job he may want?

	somewhat easier	
X	equal	
	somewhat harder	X

---

36. Now I'd like to talk with you a bit about children growing up, and the things that happen.

What sorts of things has _____ (son) done that have made you angry, upset, or disappointed in him?

Only one time. A neighbor accused him of taking a briefcase and called the detectives. My boy swore to me he had nothing to do with it. So I believed him and the detectives talked to him and were satisfied that he had nothing to do with it.

He won't stay in school. . . . He won't leave the girls alone.

---

37. Thinking of the times when _____ (son) has misbehaved in the past one or two years, what have you *usually* done about it?

He hasn't misbehaved.

Everything I possibly could. I talk to him, I try to make him feel wanted at home.

---

39. Sometimes boys do things they shouldn't do, but these things aren't very serious, just sort of wild. Sometimes they do things that are more serious. I'm going to read to you some things a boy your son's age might do. Will you tell me whether you think it was (HAND R CARD 15) . . . OK? wild but not serious? getting serious? or very serious?

Here's the first one . . .   Card 15

39a. Stealing a car, joy-riding in it, and abandoning it.

	(1)	OK	
	(2)	wild but not serious	
X	(3)	very serious	X
	(4)	don't know	

39b. Breaking into the school cafeteria at night with some friends and eating a pie.

	(1)	OK	
	(2)	wild but not serious	
	(3)	getting serious	
X	(4)	very serious	X
	(5)	don't know	

Non-Delinquent   *Repeated Delinquent*

39c. Next, breaking into school at night with some friends and throwing over wastebaskets and desks.

	(1) OK	
	(2) wild but not serious	
	(3) getting serious	
X	(4) very serious	X
	(5) don't know	

39d. And, breaking into school at night with some friends and breaking up desks and tables and smearing paint on the walls.

	(1) OK	
	(2) wild but not serious	
	(3) getting serious	
X	(4) very serious	X
	(5) don't know	

40. When _____ (son) does something he's *not* supposed to do, something you don't approve of, which of these things are you most likely to do? (HAND R CARD 16) (Put a "1" in proper space below.)

___	(1)	Spank him or hit him	1
___	(2)	Threaten to spank him or hit him	___
___	(3)	Deprive him of something he likes, like a treat or privilege	___
___	(4)	Scold him, yell at him	___
___	(5)	Tell him or show him you are disappointed in him	___
1	(6)	Point out how he should behave, talk it over	2
2	(7)	Show no feeling about it	___
___	(8)	Just wait until he does what you want, then praise him	___

41. What sorts of things has _____ (son) done that you have liked very much, things you were glad he did?

He won't take money himself un-less I give it to him. He's courteous. . . . When he wants a dollar I say, "My billfold is on my chest, go take." But he brings it to me to take out a dollar and give it to him.

The days he stays out of trouble.

46. Do you as a parent try to influence your son in his choice of friends?

X   Yes   X
         No

Non-Delinquent   *Repeated Delinquent*

47. How much influence would you say you have in your son's selection of friends? (HAND R CARD 19)

       X   (1) a great deal
                (2) some
                (3) very little
                (4) almost none   X

---

48. Do you think it makes a difference whether or not your son has any friends who have ever been picked up by the police?

                  Yes   X
       X   No

(IF YES)

48a. In what ways?

(Inap.)   I don't want him running with them.

---

49. No boy grows up without getting into trouble of one sort or another. That's part of growing up. What do you think is the most serious trouble _____ (son) has gotten into so far? What happened?

He was playing ball in the other neighborhood—where we used to live. He broke a window so he came and told me about it.	He stole a car just today. They called me just before. They took him down to the Juvenile Home. He's there now.

49a. Why do you think it happened?

It was an accident.	Oh, he thinks he's a big shot. I can't talk to him—he's so smart-acting.

49b. What did you do?

I put in a new window and told him not to play there.	(Inap.)

49g. Do you expect problems of this sort and others will keep coming up?

                  Yes
       X   No   X

Non-Delinquent　　　　　　　　　　*Repeated Delinquent*

49h. What makes you guess they will (won't)?

Accidents happen. He told me he would try not to let it happen again.	He's got a lot of good in him. Some kids have to learn the hard way.

---

50. When children get into trouble around town in Flint, do you think it is handled in a good way?

X	Yes	
	No	I don't know

50a. Why do you say that?

The law must be good for these things. I don't really know, I haven't had any really serious trouble.	(Inap.)

---

51. What do you think a parent like yourself should do if your boy stole a car, went joy-riding in it, and abandoned it?

Turn him over to law.	The law should handle it. I didn't tell him to take it!

---

52. What do you think the police should do with a boy they've picked up for stealing a car, joy-riding in it, and abandoning it?

They should punish them.	Use their own judgment about it.

---

53. Most parents disagree sometimes about how the children should be handled. About how often would you say that you and your wife disagree about this? (HAND R CARD 20)

	(1) quite often	
X	(2) sometimes	X
	(3) hardly ever	
	(4) never	

53a. What are the things you don't agree on?
(BE SURE TO GET WHO TAKES WHICH POSITION)

I tell kids some things and she doesn't want me to. . . . I tell her not to let him play sports so much.	She wants to give them too many privileges.

Non-Delinquent   *Repeated Delinquent*

53b. What other things might you disagree on?

On their meals. The kids are   Sometimes I'm too rough with them,
fussy. I tell her to tell the kids   and she doesn't like that.
that that is all there is to eat,
so eat it.

54. Husbands and wives may often disagree about things. When you and
your wife disagree about something, who has the final say in the decision?

54a. For example, if you and your wife disagreed about where to go for
a vacation, who would have the final say? (HAND R CARD 21)

       (1) wife always
       (2) wife usually, husband sometimes
  X   (3) wife and husband about the same
       (4) husband usually, wife sometimes   X
       (5) husband always

54b. Suppose you disagreed about which doctor to call when someone
was ill, who would have the final say?

  X   (1) wife always   X
       (2) wife usually, husband sometimes
       (3) wife and husband about the same
       (4) husband usually, wife sometimes
       (5) husband always

54c. . . . about your wife taking a job or a different job?

  X   (1) wife always
       (2) wife usually, husband sometimes
       (3) wife and husband about the same
       (4) husband usually, wife sometimes
       (5) husband always   X

54d. . . . about which car to buy?

  X   (1) wife always
       (2) wife usually, husband sometimes
       (3) wife and husband about the same
       (4) husband usually, wife sometimes
       (5) husband always   X

54e. . . . about how much money to spend on food for the family?

  X   (1) wife always
       (2) wife usually, husband sometimes
       (3) wife and husband about the same
       (4) husband usually, wife sometimes
       (5) husband always   X

Non-Delinquent   *Repeated Delinquent*

54f. . . . about giving your son permission to do something?

    (1) wife always
    (2) wife usually, husband sometimes
    (3) wife and husband about the same   X
    (4) husband usually, wife sometimes
X   (5) husband always

54g. . . . about which new house or apartment to move to?

X   (1) wife always
    (2) wife usually, husband sometimes   X
    (3) wife and husband about the same
    (4) husband usually, wife sometimes
    (5) husband always

54h. . . . about buying life insurance?

    (1) wife always
    (2) wife usually, husband sometimes
    (3) wife and husband about the same
    (4) husband usually, wife sometimes
X   (5) husband always   X

54i. . . . about you changing your job?

    (1) wife always   X
    (2) wife usually, husband sometimes
    (3) wife and husband about the same
    (4) husband usually, wife sometimes
X   (5) husband always

---

55. When you think of how your son should do things or what he ought to do
    . . . do you feel that you and _____ (son) agree?   (HAND R CARD 22)

    X   (1) always
        (2) usually
        (3) sometimes
        (4) seldom   X
        (5) never

---

56. Where were you born? (If U.S. get city and state; if elsewhere, get
    country).

    Iran   T_____ , Missouri

---

57. What is your birthdate?

    December 9, 1908   1911. September 15, 1911.

58. What was the highest grade of school you completed?

Oh . . . the fifth grade here.   Fourth grade.

---

59. Did you grow up on a farm, or in a small town, or city, or what?

In B_____ . This is a   In a small town. (I: where?)
small town in Iran.   K_____ , Arkansas.

---

62. What was your total family income in 1957, before taxes and consider-
ing all sources such as rents, profits, wages, interest, and so on?
Which of the boxes on this card would you put your family in?
(HAND R CARD 23)

About eight thousand dollars.   Between six and seven thousand.

A discussion of the responses in this set of interviews as they
pertain to the study's hypotheses will give the reader some idea of
how ninety-three sets of interviews were used to test hypotheses.
The discussion organizes hypotheses into three broad areas, parallel
to the organization of the next three chapters. Discussed in order
are provocations toward and controls against delinquency related to:
(1) the attitudes of boys toward their community and neighborhoods,
especially as affected by the quality of recreational and educational
facilities in their neighborhoods, (2) boys' feelings about their families, especially about their fathers, and (3) boys' perceptions of
their job futures.

While the boys shared the same community, Flint, they did
not share the same or even comparable neighborhoods. The man
and woman who interviewed the parents of non-delinquent Phil agreed
that Phil's home was in a middle-class neighborhood; the woman
who interviewed the mother of repeated delinquent Jimmy noted that
his house was "in a poor neighborhood." This neighborhood difference is confirmed by data from the 1950 U.S. Census on Housing in
the two elementary school districts: while about 80 per cent of homes
are owned by residents in both neighborhoods, the assessed value of
the homes in Phil's neighborhood is on the average several thousand
dollars higher than in Jimmy's. Also, the small proportion of rent-
ers in Phil's neighborhood paid about 20 per cent more rent in 1950
than did Jimmy's renting neighbors. The fact that Phil's family
could afford a home in a better neighborhood, even though his father and Jimmy's worked at comparable jobs in the same company,
is probably due to Phil's mother holding a full-time job, bringing in

a second income which "helps to provide many things [they] couldn't otherwise have."

The social status difference between their neighborhoods is reflected in the quality of neighborhood recreational and educational facilities. Less land has been set aside for recreation in Phil's elementary school district than in Jimmy's, but the facility is clearly better developed in Phil's. Phil has more recreational buildings easily available to him and more formal outdoor recreation spaces like a baseball diamond and an ice skating rink. Further, Flint recreation supervisors told researcher Kersten that the program and leadership provided in Phil's elementary school district were superior to those provided in Jimmy's. Phil's district ranked twelfth among Flint's thirty-five school districts on recreation facility development, while Jimmy's ranked twenty-sixth.

The junior high schools the boys were attending when they were interviewed—Phil is at this writing in high school and Jimmy in a state institution for juvenile offenders—and the elementary schools they had attended were all about thirty-five years old. There were no appreciable differences in the sizes of the classes at their schools, class loads averaging slightly over thirty pupils per teacher. Differences are apparent in some rough indices of teacher quality, however. The teachers in Phil's elementary school had on the average six more years of experience than those in Jimmy's. Related to this difference in experience is a difference in average salary for teachers at the two schools, Phil's teachers receiving about $300 more each year. Another related fact is that from 1953 to 1957 six teachers resigned their posts at Phil's school to teach elsewhere, while eighteen teachers left Jimmy's school for other teaching positions. So it is likely that Phil had more experienced, better paid, more satisfied elementary school teachers than did Jimmy. The relationship between this information about teachers and the social status of the schools in which they teach is discussed more fully in Chapter V.

Differences in the quality of recreational and educational facilities in their neighborhoods may have created differences in the boys' attitudes. Both said that "good and bad things are about equal" in the total Flint community, but non-delinquent Phil rated his own neighborhood higher than Jimmy rated his. Congeniality of neighbors seemed to be an important factor in both boys' judgments of their neighborhoods, as it was for most of the boys and parents interviewed. One of the things Jimmy liked about his neighborhood was a place to play basketball, but he didn't think there were generally good places to hang around or play in near his home. Jimmy thought his neighborhood was "worse than most" in Flint in respect to places to play, while his non-delinquent match rated his own neighborhood as "better than most" around town.

Jimmy didn't like school; Phil did. When asked why they felt as they did, Phil seemed to regard school as the conveyor belt to his future, and Jim said he didn't like some of his teachers. Their different levels of school performance may have had something to do with their feelings toward school: Phil mentioned getting good grades regularly and his record indeed showed above-average marks; Jimmy's grades were well below average.

In general, then, non-delinquent Phil had better recreational and educational facilities available to him and was more positive toward his neighborhood and school than repeated delinquent Jimmy. It seems likely that neighborhood and school were potentially stronger social controls for the one than the other.

Family was clearly more attractive to the non-delinquent than to the repeated delinquent. Phil told his interviewer that he took his personal problems to his older sister; Jimmy said that "between my mother and father—I never talk to them about my problems" and mentioned no one else. Jimmy reported less agreement with his parents than Phil did and no participation with them in any sort of activity. Apparently Jimmy's conversations with his father may have been less satisfactory since the father pointedly declined to name the major topic. When the two boys were asked on the paper-and-pencil questionnaire if they would "like to be the kind of person (your) father is," Phil was "sure" he would, and Jimmy "thought" he would. When the two boys compared their own interests with their fathers' interests, Phil reported eleven mutual interests out of fifteen possible, Jimmy only four.

Phil's and Jimmy's mothers reported using the same discipline techniques, the common "deprivation of privileges," but their fathers differed in ways which would make Phil's father more attractive to his son. Phil reported that he was never punished, a report that his father confirmed: Phil's father "talked to him" when necessary. Jimmy said he usually was not punished because he wasn't home enough. On the other hand, when he was punished by his father, the father said Jimmy was usually hit. "Hit" may be too mild a description; Jimmy's mother declined to say what it was that she and her husband disagreed about "very often," but Jimmy's father acknowledged that his wife thought he was "too rough" with their children.

There is at least one factor which would, according to the hypotheses advanced in Chapter II, make Jimmy's father more attractive to his son than Phil's to his. Jimmy gauged his father's influence over family decisions as a good deal greater than his mother's, while Phil perceived his parents as sharing all decisions asked about. Similarly, Jimmy's father reported himself more influential than does Phil's father, who actually ceded to his wife more influence over the decisions cited. On the other hand, the report is reversed when mothers' responses are considered; according to their report, Phil's father was the more influential. This type of picture of family group power will be discussed more fully in Chapter VII.

When asked whom he would want to be like, Phil quickly replied, " . . . my next-door neighbor," who "had a good job and was nice to his little boy"; Jimmy had no model in mind. The interviewer presented the boys with the alternative models, two singers well known to teen-agers, Pat Boone and Elvis Presley. Boone and Presley represent quite different cultures; in the phrases of W. L. Whyte (1943), Boone is a "college boy" and Presley, a "corner boy." The jacket designs on two of their record releases, current during the field research work, nicely illustrate this difference: Boone's design is an arrangement of college symbols—pennant, racoon coat, white buck shoes, etc.—and Boone was in fact a student at Columbia University at the time; Presley's design is an impression of the singer strumming his guitar behind cell bars, in connection with his appearance in a motion picture, "Jail-house Rock." Phil chose Boone; Jimmy chose Presley.

To check on the social control potential of each boy's model, each was asked how his model would react to some specific delinquent behaviors. Phil's "next-door neighbor" regarded all three behaviors as "very serious"; Jimmy's "Presley" image thought one of them was "wild but not serious." But Jimmy's emotions seem to have been touched by the recital of delinquent acts: Jimmy laughed and responded sarcastically at that part in the interview, perhaps to insist that, compared to his own record, the behaviors mentioned were really child's play.

The two boys seemed oriented toward different goals in their futures. For Phil, "success" meant having friends and constant striving; for Jimmy, "success" meant "having everything you want." Phil reported having thought more about the kind of occupation he wanted to pursue and had his sights on being either a lawyer or a chiropractor. Status seems to have been important in Phil's choice: he mentioned that either of his aspirations was "respectable." Phil's parents also seemed to have some profession in mind for their son.

Some confusion surrounded Jimmy's job aspirations. He himself said he wanted to begin working as a grocer's boy, then perhaps buy the store and develop a chain of stores, or maybe go into the restaurant business. But both of Jimmy's parents had the impression their son was headed toward becoming a "hairdresser" or "barber." While non-delinquent Phil recognized that the path to his aspiration led through school, repeated delinquent Jimmy saw only a first step, getting a store clerk job, through knowing the owner.

Their fathers were occupational role models for neither boy. Both Phil and Jim believed their fathers disliked their jobs and wanted businesses of their own, although neither father expressed this desire. Phil did have models close at hand, however, in his brother-in-law and in a family friend; Jimmy mentioned no model and asserted that most of the people he knew disliked their jobs.

So there seem to have been several differences in the boys' aspirations: Phil's was higher than Jimmy's on a society-wide scale of prestige; Phil seems to have had his goal fairly clearly defined, while Jimmy seems to have been clear neither in himself nor to his parents; Phil seems to have anticipated more pleasure in the process of gaining and having gained his goal, while Jimmy projected a picture of jobs as not pleasurable but rather as means to get things you want.

Phil estimated his chances at getting the job he wanted as "fair," while Jimmy seems to have been more sure of reaching his goal. Their mothers were both conservative in their estimates, and their fathers optimistic. Phil was not sure if a delinquent record would have made any difference in his chances; Jimmy felt a delinquent record does make a difference, but his own seven contacts apparently did not lead him to lower his estimate for himself.

It is difficult to say whether Jimmy had a greater status problem than Phil which might have provoked the former to delinquency. Jimmy did project a prestigeful future image of himself as an owner of a chain of groceries or as a restauranteur. But the image is a fuzzy one; Jimmy's parents apparently didn't get it. Furthermore, Jimmy made a strange judgment when he was asked to rate the quality of different jobs as other people saw them: he rated "store clerk" higher than "judge," "advertising executive," and "chemical engineer." One wonders if Jimmy was not being defensive about his future. In any case, when asked how he felt about his future generally, Jimmy was not so optimistic as Phil.

The foregoing analysis of one set of responses does not exploit all the information available in the records. Undoubtedly the reader has some hunches about the meaning of responses which were not discussed in the commentary. A more complete exploitation of the data is reported in the next four chapters, where data from ninety-three sets of records have been compiled and subjected to statistical analysis. While the source in the interview schedule of each item of data will be cited as findings are reported, it will be helpful for the sake of context to keep in mind the total picture illustrated by Phil, Jimmy, and their parents. It is from reading whole records like these that one gets the impression that not one factor underlies juvenile delinquency but a pattern of forces operating in a boy's life situation.

Chapter V

RECREATIONAL AND EDUCATIONAL FACILITIES
AS SOURCES OF DELINQUENCY CONTROL

Central to the theory of delinquency which was tested in this study is the idea that a social organization like the Flint community can effectively control its members, like its teen-age boys, to the degree that it is attractive to those members. Because it may be especially relevant to youngsters' attraction to their community, one of the possible links of juvenile delinquency to social status is the quality of the recreational and educational facilities offered to youngsters by their community. If the quality of these facilities differs from neighborhoods of one social status to neighborhoods of another, this may result in differences in youngsters' attractions to their community and consequent differences in the extent to which their community can influence them to accept its standards of behavior.

Previous research on delinquency demonstrates clearly that delinquents relate differently to their schools than do non-delinquents, but differences are not so clear-cut in the area of recreation. On the subject of recreation, sociologist M. H. Neumeyer wrote, in his 1949 text on delinquency, "The inadequacy of recreation facilities and programs in communities may be considered as a condition of delinquency" (1949, p. 158). On the other hand, in his text of the same year, sociologist P. W. Tappan stated, "Proof that active or guided recreation itself prevents delinquency or that its absence causes misbehavior is lacking" (1949, p. 149).

At least two sets of data have been reported which show that delinquents are not so often involved in organized recreation. The Gluecks (*op. cit.*) found that 61 per cent of their non-delinquents reported having spent leisure hours at playgrounds, compared to 29 per cent of their institutionalized delinquents, who more often had hung around on street corners, in vacant lots, and in poolrooms. A report by E. Shanas (1942) for the Chicago Recreation Commission reveals that in 1938-39, more non-delinquent boys utilized formal recreation areas than boys with police and/or court records. The proportions of recreation facility users in the four sections of

107

Chicago studied ranged from 63 per cent to 96 per cent of non-delinquents and from 41 per cent to 61 per cent of official delinquents.

On the other hand, Thrasher (1936) found that as many delinquents as non-delinquents participated in a Boys' Club recreational program in a Brooklyn neighborhood, but that this participation seemed to have no effect on the incidence of delinquent behavior.

A question arises about the reasons behind these findings relating recreation to delinquency. Do delinquents use recreational facilities less because they are not so available or because the delinquents are not so inclined? Shanas' work suggests it is a matter of inclination; Shanas sampled not delinquents but recreation areas equally available to delinquents and non-delinquents in the vicinity, and she found that fewer delinquents appeared at them. Yet delinquents' lack of motivation to use recreational facilities probably does not indicate less interest in the kinds of recreation offered; for Healy's and Bronner's (*op. cit.*) data show that compared to their non-delinquent siblings, delinquents are more interested in and more skillful at sports. Data from the Glueck study suggest that it is the element of supervision at formal recreation areas which repels delinquents: in the judgment of the interviewing psychiatrist, 21 per cent of the institutionalized delinquents disdained supervised recreation, compared to 12 per cent of the non-delinquents.

Many studies have found that delinquents differ from non-delinquents in many ways related to school. The Gluecks (*op. cit.*) found a "marked dislike of school" among 62 per cent of their institutionalized delinquents and 10 per cent of their non-delinquent matched controls; W. W. Wattenberg (1947) got essentially the same results comparing Detroit boys with repeated police contacts to boys with only one contact; and Healy and Bronner (*op. cit.*) report the same difference in attitudes toward school between delinquent and non-delinquent sibs. Further, the Gluecks (*op. cit.*) and Kvaraceus (1945) found delinquents have poorer school achievement records than non-delinquent controls.

Recreational and Educational Facilities and Delinquency: Theory

It has been suggested that differences in the quality of recreational and educational facilities from one neighborhood to another are important factors in the process which links the incidence of juvenile delinquency to social status. The process begins with the fact that (1) lower status neighborhoods have facilities of poorer quality; then (2) poorer quality facilities weaken attraction to the community and its institutions; and finally, (3) weak attraction to the community and its institutions raises the probability of delinquent behavior. The result is that delinquency occurs more often among lower status youngsters, which is the fact this research was intended to explain.

A "because" statement is implied in each link in the process-chain. Two have already been discussed. Poorer quality facilities lead to weak attractions because the attraction individuals feel toward a social organization depend upon the ability of the organization to satisfy the desires of the individual, in this case a youngster's desires for recreation and adequate education. Weak attraction raises the possibility of delinquent behavior because weak attraction can support only weak social controls which may give way before whatever provocations are operating to encourage delinquency.

Neighborhood Social Status and Recreational Facilities

Why do lower status neighborhoods have poorer facilities? The reasons for this phenomenon are discussed after its existence is investigated. A brief review of the nature of the data involved here is in order. The social status of a neighborhood is measured by indices constructed for each elementary school district from figures compiled during the 1950 U.S. Census on Housing. There are three indices: the *proportion of owners* in the district; the *average value of dwelling units*; and the product of the first two, called the *weighted value*. It has been pointed out that proportion of owners emphasizes city expansion away from its older, commercial center, while average value of dwelling units roughly describes the distribution of wealth about Flint.

The quality of recreational facilities was determined by L. Kersten (1958), who personally visited each youth-serving public recreation space and rated it on several dimensions. His data yielded measures of *land allotment*, the acreage provided for playspace in each district, including school and park facilities; *land use*, a point-system Kersten invented to summarize and standardize information on the presence of recreation structures, physical equipment, formally laid out playspace, and leadership and program as rated by recreation supervisors; and a *general* measure, the sum of the first two.

The construction of other measures used in this chapter have already been described in detail: the quality of educational facilities, based on information from the Flint Board of Education and its accounting office; delinquency rates by elementary school district; the interview items measuring boys' attractions to Flint and their neighborhoods; and the categorization of boys as repeated or non-delinquents. In this chapter and in the two which follow, comparisons are made only between repeated delinquents and non-delinquents. Comparisons involving sometime delinquents are all discussed in Chapter VIII.

The first process-link to be discussed is the relationship between the social statuses of Flint elementary school districts and the quality of their recreational facilities. It was hypothesized that lower status neighborhoods have poorer facilities. To test this hypothesis, elementary school districts were ranked from high to low on each of the three social status measures and on each of the recreation indices. A rank-order statistic, *tau* (Siegel, *op. cit.*), was applied to gauge the extent to which rank orders were similar. Table A-5 contains the results of this analysis. The rank order on average value does not seem to be related reliably to the rank order on land allotment. (In this study, relationships were considered reliable if by chance they could have occurred in the predicted direction only five times out of a hundred.)

On the other hand, the coefficients of .27 between average value and land use and .25 between average value and the general index could have occurred by chance only twice in 100 times, so they most likely reveal an actual, reliable relationship. In this case, the higher the average value of dwelling units in a neighborhood, the better developed the facility tended to be. A closer analysis of these data, not presented here, indicates that the leadership and program components of land use are most closely related to average value.

Proportion of owners, as a social status index, shows a different pattern from average value. Table A-5 shows that proportion of owners is highly reliably related to land allotment and probably not related to land use. Weighted value, the over-all social status index, is reliably related to two of the three indices of the quality of recreational facilities, which is to be expected, since components of weighted value are related to one or another of the recreation indices.

These figures suggest an understandable relationship between social status and recreational indices. Land allotment is high where proportion of owners is high probably because proportion of owners, related as it is to city expansion, is high on the edges of Flint where there is more land available for public playspace. Land allotment is low toward the center of Flint where proportion of owners is relatively low, probably for two reasons: first, the whole concept of city parks and school playgrounds was not so compelling in the time when Flint was young, so less land was originally set aside for recreation.   Even by a measure of acreage-per-child, there is less land allotted for recreation where the proportion of home owners is low, nearer the center of Flint.

Recreation facilities tend to be more developed where the average values of homes is high partly for the same historical reasons which relate newer homes to better facilities, since newer homes generally carry higher average values.   But probably this explanation does not account for all the relationship because there are newer, lower status neighborhoods in Flint which have poorer recreation facilities than older, higher status neighborhoods.   One might speculate that influence is also a factor: wealthier citizens have composed the more stable political force in Flint as elsewhere and comprise the population from which most office-holding policy makers have been drawn.   So when limited public resources can be invested only in limited areas, wealthier areas dominate the competition for public facilities.   Flint is not unique in respect to this phenomenon.   In whatever way differences are established in the quality of recreational facilities from higher to lower status neighborhoods, these differences seem to exist.

Boys' Attitudes and Recreational Facilities

The next link discussed is that which joins the quality of facilities to boys' attitudes toward Flint and their neighborhoods. Boys' answers to the question, "How do you feel about Flint?" bear no reliable relationship to the quality of the recreational facilities in their neighborhoods.   But, as Table 8 demonstrates, their responses to the question, "How do you feel about the neighborhood where you live?" tend to be more negative where recreational facilities are poorer in quality.   Because leadership and program components of land use appeared most closely associated to the social status indicator, the measure of land use was pulled apart in this analysis to reveal components operating separately.   It seems that the quality of leadership and program is also the most closely related to boys' attitudes toward their neighborhoods.   So far the data suggest that the quality of recreational facilities may shape boys' attractions to their neighborhoods, but probably not to Flint as a

whole; and possibly the strongest factor which determines their attractions, the human resources of recreational leadership and program rather than land or physical resources, is also most closely
tied to the social status of their neighborhoods.

Table 8

When the relationship between quality of neighborhood recreation
facilities and boys' attitudes toward aspects of their community
is investigated, more attitudes toward neighborhood are negative
in school districts with poorer facilities.

Question 2: How do you feel about the neighborhood where you live ?

RECREATIONAL FACILITIES	RELATIVE QUALITY OF RECREATIONAL FACILITIES	ATTITUDE TOWARD NEIGHBORHOOD		
		A very good place	A good place	So-so to very bad place
IN LAND	High	54	28	18 (N=83)
	Average	45	24	31 (78)
	Low	51	20	29 (45)
IN BUILDINGS AND EQUIPMENT	High	60	21	18 (71)
	Average	40	30	30 (100)
	Low	57	17	26 (35)
IN LEADERSHIP AND PROGRAM	High	68	14	18 (50)
	Average	41	32	27 (95)
	Low	49	23	28 (61)

   The third and last link in the process-chain is the relationship between boys' attractions to the community and neighborhood
and their behavior.   It was hypothesized that repeated delinquents
would exhibit more negative attitudes than their non-delinquent
matched controls.   The test of this hypothesis utilized the core sample of boys.   Each repeated delinquent was compared to his match,
and the size and direction of the difference in their attitudes were
noted.   A statistical technique designed to test differences in matched
samples, the t-test for correlated means (Blalock, 1960, p. 179)
was applied to these data to determine if reliable differences occurred.   The data in Table 9 confirm the hypothesis: repeated delinquents are more negative toward Flint and toward their neighborhoods.   They tend to be more negative at each social status level.

Table 9

Repeated delinquents tend to regard their community and neighborhood less favorably than matched non-delinquents.

☐ Non-Delinquents (N=93)   ▨ Repeated Delinquents (N=93)

Question I: How do you feel about Flint ?   Question 2: How do you feel about your neighborhood ?

A very good place (1)
19 %
30%
45%
56%

More good than bad things (2)
42%
32%
23%
28%

Good and bad things about equal (3)
30%
36%
25%
13%

More bad than good things (4)
8%
2%
5%
3%

A very bad place (5)
1%
0%
2%
0%

	White Collar		Skilled		Unskilled		Total			White Collar		Skilled		Unskilled		Total	
	Repeaters	Non-del.	Repeaters	Non-del.	Repeaters	Non-del.	Repeaters	Non-del.		Repeaters	Non-del.	Repeaters	Non-del.	Repeaters	Non-del.	Repeaters	Non-del.
Mean	2.2	1.8	2.5	2.2	2.2	2.2	2.3	2.1	Mean	1.7	1.7	1.7	1.4	2.0	1.8	2.0	1.6
N	20		27		46		93		N	20		27		46		93	
t	1.9		1.0		0.4		1.5		t	0.2		2.4		1.1		2.2	
p	<.03		NR		NR		<.05		p	NR		<.01		NR		<.01	

The entries in Table 9 are the percentages of repeated delinquents and non-delinquents who gave each response. They show, for example, that more repeated delinquents responded unfavorably to Flint, only 19 per cent of them choosing the alternative "a very good place," compared to 30 per cent of the non-delinquents. The t-test (for correlated means) summary beneath each set of responses gives the mean scores of the matched groups, the N, number of pairs in the t analysis, and the one-tailed probability of the differences between the means being reliably different. In Table 9, 93 pairs, or all the boys, answered in some codeable way to the question,

"How do you feel about Flint?" Assigning a score of 1 for the re-sponse, "a very good place" to a score of 5 for "a very bad place," the means for the white collar repeaters and non-delinquents are 2.2 and 1.8 respectively. This difference of 0.4, with the repeaters less favorable, as expected, could have occurred by chance only 3 times out of 100, which is sufficiently reliable to consider the dif-ference as an other-than-chance event.

Since negative attitudes toward the neighborhood are related on the one hand to relatively poor recreation facilities and on the other hand to repeated delinquency, it is probable then that areas of poorer recreational facilities have higher delinquency rates. This relationship was tested by rank-ordering elementary school districts on each of the three indices of the quality of recreational facilities to compare with the rank order on delinquency rates. Table 10 presents the results of the test: reliable negative relationships ap-pear between quality indices and the delinquency rate, the higher the quality of facilities, the lower the delinquency rate.

Table 10

The poorer the quality of recreational facilities in an elementary school district, the higher the delinquency rate is likely to be in that district.

Delinquency Rate (white male, 1957) x	τ	p-level (1t)
Recreation index:		
Land allotment	-.22	.04
Land use	-.24	.03
General	-.27	.02

So the data lend credence to the hypothetical process linking social status to delinquency through recreational facilities. The data especially emphasize the importance of recreational leadership and program in this process.

But the results of a close test of one link in the process-chain suggest some modification of the picture which has emerged thus far. The link between the quality of recreational facilities and atti-tudes toward the neighborhood seems to be specific to repeated de-linquents. The first demonstration of this relationship, in Table 10, combined delinquents and non-delinquents; the analysis summarized in Table 11 separated them. A measure of covariation, K. Pear-son's correlation coefficient, r, was applied to the data, with the result that reliable relationships appeared between the quality of recreational facilities and the attitudes of repeated delinquents only. Furthermore, the primacy of leadership and program disappeared, except where it occurred unreliably among non-delinquents. Thus, a general statement that poor recreational facilities weaken boys' attractions to their neighborhoods is probably not true; rather, poor facilities weaken attractions felt by repeated delinquents. This phenomenon is discussed further after parallel data concerning school facilities are presented.

Table 11

The attitudes of repeated delinquents toward recreational facilities in their neighborhoods are more closely related to the quality of those facilities than are the attitudes of non-delinquents.

Attitude toward Recreational Facilities x	Repeated Delinquents		Non-Delinquents	
	r	p-level (1t)	r	p-level (1t)
Land allotted.	.18	<.05	.00	NR
Buildings and equipment.	.26	<.01	.02	NR
Leadership program	.21	<.03	.16	NR
General	.27	<.01	.05	NR

Neighborhood Social Status and School Facilities

The reasoning behind hypotheses relating the quality of school facilities to social status and to delinquency is similar to the reasoning about recreational facilities. The first link tested was the one between the quality of school facilities and the social status of neighborhoods. The results of this test are presented in Table 12. The first column in Table 12 contains the relationships between three indices of the quality of educational facilities on the elementary school level and one social status index, average value. Only teachers' average salary shows a reliable relationship to average value, a rank-order correlation of .42, possible by chance five times out of ten thousand. The relationship is positive; that is, the higher the social status of the school district, the higher teachers' average salary tends to be. The third column contains correlations between proportion of home owners and the quality indices. Here, only age of school is reliably related to the social status index; the positive correlation, .56, indicates that the newer the school, the higher the proportion of owners in the district. The summary social status index, weighted value, is reliably related both to teachers' average salary and age of school because one or another of its components is.

Table 12

Teachers are better paid in elementary schools surrounded by neighborhoods with high property values; schools are newer in areas where greater proportions of people own their homes; the crowdedness of classrooms is not related to socio-economic indices.

Education Indices	Socio-economic Indices					
	Value of Dwelling Units		Per Cent Owners		Weighted Value	
	τ	p-level (1t)	τ	p-level (1t)	τ	p-level (1t)
Teachers' average salary	.42	.0005	.10	.21	.40	.0008
Age of school	.05	.48	.56	.00003	.43	.0003
Class load	.08	.27	.04	.38	.05	.34

Summing the components into weighted values produces lower correlations, which indicate weaker relationships and suggests that the two components of social status are operating independently.

Class loads are unrelated to social status indices. The newer families which make up the bulk of the expansion at the edges of cities appear to be populating Flint elementary schoolrooms as fast as they can be built.

The results of this analysis of data on educational facilities are strikingly similar to those concerning recreational facilities: the quality of the physical plant, the school in this case, is related to the index describing city expansion; the quality of the personnel, here indicated by teachers' average salary, is related to the index describing the distribution of wealth. The process which may lie behind this pattern of relationships seems more apparent in the case of school facilities and is discussed in this context; then implications back to recreational facilities are drawn.

Teaching Staff and the Social Status of the School District

The puzzle is not in the relationship of age of school to city expansion. The explanation for this relationship is obvious. But why does the quality of a teaching staff tend to be lower in areas of less wealth?

Perhaps the first point to justify is the assumption that lower average salary is an index of a poorer quality teaching staff. This assumption rests initially on the fact that in the Flint school system, as in almost every school system in the United States, a teacher's salary is closely tied to the number of years of her teaching experience and to her professional training as indicated by the highest academic degree she has earned. Data not presented here reveal that teachers' salaries are indeed very closely correlated with experience and degrees earned, and the Flint Board of Education annually publishes the scale which explicitly links salaries to experience and degrees earned. The second assumption is that, overall, more experience and more training produce better teachers. Undoubtedly, there are exceptions to this assumption, but this assumption nevertheless is generally accepted by school administrators and underlies the fact that they pay higher salaries to teachers with more experience and higher degrees.

If the statement can be accepted at least tentatively that lower status elementary schools in Flint have on the average teachers of lower quality, it is reasonable to ask why. A possible explanation for this phenomenon starts out with the assumption that better teachers can, if they want to, more easily get jobs elsewhere than teachers of lower quality; that is plausible enough. The second assumption is that teachers frequently do want to get out of schools in lower status neighborhoods. Perhaps this assumption requires support. Data were obtained on the number of teacher resignations from each elementary school in the five years from 1953 to 1957. Only resignations which implied clearly that teachers could get other teaching jobs were included; resignations for reasons of retirement, illness, maternity, and marriage were not counted. Schools were then ranked on the number of resignations, and this rank order was compared to the rank order on the average value index of social status. The similarity of the rank orders could have occurred by chance only twice out of 1,000 times. More teachers resigned from elementary schools serving lower status neighborhoods. It seems, then, that turnover accounts for the generally lower quality of teachers in lower status schools. An examination of the data revealed that teachers who resigned and left the Flint school system accounted for this relationship; turnover resulting from transfers to other Flint schools was not concentrated in lower status school districts.

It should not be assumed that this relationship is rare, perhaps even unique to Flint. At least one other researcher confirmed these findings for another city. P. C. Sexton (1960) found that in Detroit's public school system, "emergency regular substitute teachers," teachers lacking the state's minimum teaching qualifications, were reliably more often employed in lower status schools.

Sexton's study is a useful complement to the present research, since it includes data beyond the elementary school level. It was not feasible to relate data from Flint junior and senior high schools to neighborhood social status indices since these schools serve larger, socially heterogeneous areas of Flint, and, indeed, students from anywhere in town could at the time of this study choose which of the three Flint high schools they wished to attend. But in the larger city of Detroit, each "sub-community," served by several junior and senior high schools, is socially more uniform. Sexton's measure of social status was the average income of residents in each sub-community; she obtained data on school facilities from a current large-scale citizens' study of Detroit schools.

Sexton's Detroit data generally repeat the present findings for Flint. For example, one-third of the Detroit elementary school children from neighborhoods with an average salary less than $7,000 attend schools over fifty years old; no children from wealthier neighborhoods attend schools so old. Sexton also reported data demonstrating that secondary schools are less adequate in lower status neighborhoods. As in Flint, class loads in Detroit are not related to the social status of school districts.

It seems reasonable to conclude that school facilities are poorer in quality in lower status neighborhoods. Since recreational facilities show the same relationship to social status, the pattern appears to be that lower status youngsters have less adequate educational and recreational facilities in their neighborhoods. Table 13

Table 13

Better teachers' salaries and better development of recreation facilities and program tend to go together in Flint elementary school districts; schools tend to be older in those school districts where there is less land allotted for recreation.

| Education Indices | Recreation Indices | | | | | |
| | Land | | Land Use | | General | |
	τ	p-level (1t)	τ	p-level (1t)	τ	p-level (1t)
Teachers' average salary. . . .	.14	.13	.23	.04	.27	.02
Age of school	.37	.002	-.004	.49	.18	.08
Class load	.06	.31	.10	.21	.14	.13

bears this out: where teachers' average salary is low, recreational land use tends to be less adequate; where schools are old, less land is set aside for recreation. Older schools and less recreational acreage are both outcomes of city expansion patterns. It has been suggested that the lower quality of teaching staffs in lower status schools is due to better teachers leaving them for jobs elsewhere; perhaps a similar process partly determines the less adequate use of recreational land in lower status neighborhoods, since the leadership and program component of land use is most closely related to social status. Unfortunately, data were not available on turnover among recreation leaders.

Boys' Attitudes and School Facilities

What effect does a poorer quality of educational facilities have on boys' attitudes toward their community and their neighborhoods? This was the next link tested. The results are negative. Boys' attitudes do not seem to be reliably related to the age of their schools, the average salary of their teachers, or the size of their classes.

Furthermore, the corresponding link between attitudes and the quality of recreational facilities has also been found to be weak. The data do not support the hypothesis that the quality of educational and recreational facilities significantly affect boys' attitudes toward Flint or their neighborhoods.

School Facilities and Delinquency

Nevertheless, it seems that where school facilities are poorer, delinquency rates are higher. Table 14 shows that the higher the average salary of elementary school teachers, the lower the delinquency rate in the neighborhood served by the school, and the newer the school, the lower the rate. With the attitude link missing, however, it seems most likely that the quality of school facilities is related to delinquency rates because both are related to neighborhood social status. That is, social status is affecting both factors, and these factors are not in themselves related. A statistical technique, partial correlation, enables one artificially to level off the effects of social status to see if anything is left of the relationship between school facilities and delinquency. The results of this analysis, not presented here, reveal that no reliable relationship is left, supporting the conclusion that neighborhood social status is the potent factor.

Table 14

Newer schools and schools in which teachers are on the average earning higher salaries are surrounded by neighborhoods
with lower delinquency rates.

Education Indices	Rank Correlation with Delinquency Rate (male, 1957)	p-level (1t)
Teachers' average salary............	−.31	.007
Age of school	.44	.0003
Class load	.04	.37

Summary

A process-chain was hypothesized to run from social status
through the quality of recreational and educational facilities to attitudes conducive to delinquency.   The fact that it breaks down at the
point where attitudes are linked to facilities suggests that these facilities are not salient aspects of the community or neighborhoods
for the boys studied.   Perhaps boys are not even aware of the adequacy of their school buildings or of the quality of their teachers
as school administrators measure that quality.   Perhaps a vacant
lot, a drug store, a drive-in, any place to hang around is sufficient
recreation space for adolescent boys, who avoid supervised recreation generally.   Researchers on the Chicago recreation study (Shanas,
op. cit.) found that participation by boys in supervised recreation
drops off after the age of fourteen.

Still, some of the data indicate that the attitudes of repeated
delinquents toward their neighborhoods are related to the quality of
recreational facilities there.   Perhaps this finding demonstrates a
kind of scapegoating mechanism.   That is, repeated delinquents may
be looking for an object upon which to invest some of their negativ-
ism, and neighborhoods which offer poorer recreational facilities or
are generally less attractive may provide handy targets.

There is no indication in the data that repeated delinquents
actually have less access to or even utilize recreational facilities
less than do their non-delinquent controls.   Data analyzed but not
presented here show that delinquents do not differ reliably from
non-delinquents in their judgment of places to play in their neighborhoods or in their reports of how often they use public recreation space.   It is unfortunate, however, that boys' judgments of
neighborhood recreation personnel were not specifically elicited.

The last link in the hypothetical process-chain, relating nega-tive attitudes toward school with repeated delinquency, does seem to exist. The data in Tables 15 and 16 repeat the findings reported often in the literature that delinquents at all social status levels like school less well than non-delinquents and more often want to quit school. But it should be pointed out that only a small propor-tion of boys reported that they wanted to quit school, or were even

Table 15

Repeated delinquents are more likely to be negative toward school than are matched non-delinquents.

Question 19: How do you like school ?

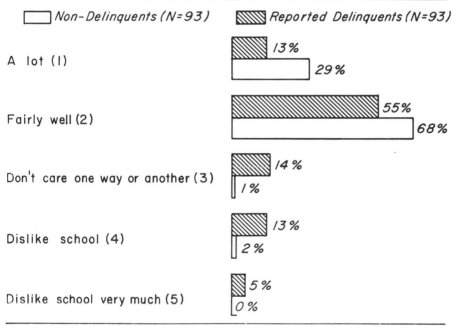

	White Collar		Skilled		Unskilled		Total	
	Repeat-ers	Non-del.	Repeat-ers	Non-del.	Repeat-ers	Non-del.	Repeat-ers	Non-del.
Mean	2.4	1.7	2.4	1.8	2.4	1.9	2.4	1.8
N	20		27		46		93	
t	4.3		3.4		2.9		5.4	
p	.0003		.003		.003		.0003	

doubtful about continuing. So, while the difference in frequency of "want to quit" responses between repeated delinquents and their matched controls is reliable, only a small proportion of pairs, 16 per cent, actually differed. The picture presented is largely one of boys tolerating school rather than abandoning it.

In summary, it seems that the quality of educational and recreational facilities does not help to explain the relationship of social status to delinquency. Yet, the facts remain that delinquent boys more often come from lower status categories, and they are less attracted to their community, neighborhoods, and schools. Another process-chain which may link these facts is investigated in the next chapter, which discusses family relationships as they are related to delinquency.

Table 16

Of the few boys who want to quit school when they are 16, more are repeated delinquents.

Question 21: Do you want to quit school when you're 16?

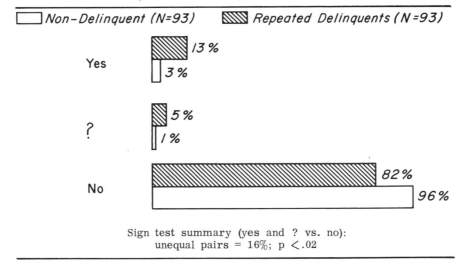

Non-Delinquent (N=93)   Repeated Delinquents (N=93)

Yes — 13% / 3%

? — 5% / 1%

No — 82% / 96%

Sign test summary (yes and ? vs. no):
unequal pairs = 16%; p < .02

Chapter VI

FAMILIES AS SOURCES OF DELINQUENCY CONTROL

Psychologists and psychiatrists have emphasized the part families play in the phenomenon of delinquency. The great majority of delinquency research with a psychological orientation has been research on family relationships. This research has shown repeatedly that the families of delinquents are somehow less adequate than those of non-delinquents: homes are broken by death, divorce, or separation; homes are "psychologically broken," that is, parents are openly hostile to one another and unhappy with their marriage; children are rejected and neglected; parents are themselves criminal and encourage delinquency in their offspring; families are living on relief checks and at the verge of complete destitution.

The police also recognize the relevance of a youngster's family to his delinquent behavior. Decisions about the disposition of his care to the court, to an institution, to a probation officer, or to his parents seem to depend largely on a judgment of the capacity of the family to control the youngster. Officials generally acknowledge that the family is the agency with the greatest potential for delinquency control and should be given the opportunity to handle their children until it becomes clear that a particular family cannot establish control. One mother reflected this police position when she commented on how authorities should handle delinquents: "If they are under age and if it's the first offense, they should be turned back to the parents, *if the parents are responsible people.*"

Probably the most popular lay theory about the cause of delinquency is also that families are somehow to blame. One mother of a non-delinquent boy in the present study justified allowing her son to associate with known delinquents by saying, "I don't think it's the boy's fault he's bad, he wasn't born bad, his family turned him that way. Maybe my boy can do him some good. We feel we've turned him to the good and he won't change that."

The thesis of this chapter rests on the assumption that the family is the primary source of social control in the life of a boy,

123

and the weaker this control, the greater the likelihood that a boy will become delinquent. It is proposed that family control, like the control any group maintains over a member, depends in part on its attractiveness for that member, especially when the member is not wholly dependent on the group to satisfy his needs. Furthermore, it is proposed here that families in lower social strata have characteristics closely related to their lower status which make them less attractive to their sons and therefore disadvantage them in establishing social control. It is this weakening of social control potential among lower status families which may help to account for higher delinquency rates among lower status boys.

Some possible reasons for the relative unattractiveness of lower status families are obvious: they do not so often live in attractive houses with recreation space and equipment for youngsters; they often cannot provide their children with the clothes, sports equipment, late-model automobile, and spending money available to children from higher status homes; a degree of companionship and supervision is lacking if both parents must work; and more lower status families are fragmented by divorce, separation, and desertion. However, less obvious elements of family attractiveness seemed both more central to the problem of control over delinquency and to the over-arching problem of the impact of social status on personality development.

Father-Son Relationships and Delinquency

The research reported here was focused primarily on the boy's relationship with his father as an important determinant of family attractiveness. This approach was taken on the assumption that the important aspects of a boy's attraction to his family group are contained in his attraction to its members, particularly his parents, and more particularly, his father. The decision to focus upon father-son relationships was largely determined by the theory of social control dominant in psychological thinking today and by empirical findings reported in the delinquency literature.

The psychoanalytic theory of social control considers conscience, or superego, as the psychic representation of social norms about behavior. The theory asserts that the superego is established in an individual through identification with authority figures, most often, through identification with one's parents. That is, for various reasons the small child wishes he were like his parents and begins to imitate them; part of his imitation of them involves his acceptance of their standards of behavior. One example of imitation in the course of identification is the frequent instance of a child admonishing himself aloud to do, or more often, not to do something in the very words and tone used by his parents toward him. As a child grows older, the outward manifestations of his identification gradually disappear, but parental images remain as the voices of conscience. Various studies have shown that among adolescents, parents are still the major source of the standards which guide behavior (e.g., Newcomb, 1943; Solomon, 1960).

According to the theory, fathers are more important than mothers in the development of superego among boys. Presumably children begin to recognize differences in the sexes at an early age and learn which parent they resemble most. Establishment of their physical similarity to their fathers, in addition to the eagerness of parents to encourage their children to behave in ways appropriate to their sex, leads most boys to select their fathers rather than their mothers to emulate. Furthermore, psychoanalytic theory proposes that every boy goes through a stage when he wishes to supplant his father in the affections of his mother, but when he is unable to take over from his father, a boy substitutes identification with him and thereby enjoys the relationship with his mother vicariously. This latter process, the resolution of the Oedipal conflict, is posited as a major reason for boys identifying with their fathers and incorporating primarily their father's standards of behavior as their own. According to psychoanalytic thinking, then, early relationships with fathers are important in the establishment of inner social control among boys.

In addition to psychological theory about the development of inner control, empirical findings in studies of delinquents and of boys in general prompted a focus on father-son relationships. The sum of the research strongly suggests that the role of fathers is crucial. A. Bandura and R. H. Walters (1959), reporting a study of boys on probation or known through school to be aggressively antisocial, wrote:

> The aggressive boys sought the help and company of their parents to a much lesser degree than did the control boys. Their lack of dependency was most evident in their relationships with their fathers [1959, pp. 70-71].

U. Bronfenbrenner (in press) studied boys and girls who were known as responsible or irresponsible citizens at school and reported that for sons, high levels of responsibility were associated with increased discipline and authority by the father; this was not true for daughters or for boys in relationship to their mothers. F. I. Nye (*op. cit.*).

found that self-admitted delinquent boys less often said they sought
advice from their fathers than did non-delinquent boys, but advice-
seeking from mothers was not related to delinquency. W. Wattenberg (*op. cit.*) reported that boy repeaters more often choose their
mothers as someone to be like than their fathers. While a study of
alleged delinquents done by the McCords (*op. cit.*) suggests that boys'
relationships with their mothers are equally important in determining delinquent behavior, the weight of the evidence stresses boys'
relationships with their fathers.

It should be pointed out, however, that the psychoanalytic theory of identification and the empirical evidence cited are not directly relevant to one another. This is because identification, as psy-
choanalytical theorists conceive of it, is largely an unconscious characteristic of personality not accessible to the kind of superficial
probing which these studies employed. It might rather be said that
the researchers were measuring surface manifestations of underlying identification processes.

The approach to father-son relationships taken in this work
was also on a relatively superficial level, in the sense that the survey interview method was not likely to tap unconscious identification
processes. The more superficial aspects of father-son relationships were conceptualized here as a special instance of the general
theory of attraction and conformity which was developed in the context of group dynamics theory and research. That is, the father-
son dyad was considered a small group in which a boy's attraction
to his father tended to make him conform to, be controlled by, his
father's wishes. Formulated in this way, sources of attraction to
fathers became a central problem for research. More specifically,
the major theme of this research required the isolation of variables
related to the attraction of fathers which depended more or less directly on their social status.

Social Status and Family Organization

One possible link to social status variables of fathers' attractiveness and the attractiveness of the family concerns the goals of
the family as a group. Those theorists who have concerned themselves with the family as a group (e.g., Burgess and Locke, 1945;
Parsons and Bales, 1955) have posited essentially two goals for it,
the satisfaction of members' basic physical and social needs and the
socialization of children. Attention has not been explicitly paid to
what may be the overriding goal of the family group, the one which
sets the standard by which the other goals are accomplished, namely,

the achievement of upward mobility. After all, status is assigned to family units. It seems to be characteristic of societies throughout the cultures of the world that family members share a common status level. Since higher status is usually regarded as a goal worth achieving and since members of a family must achieve it together, a plausible assumption is that families organize as groups to attain higher status, just as business firms organize to maximize profit or athletes organize as teams to win games. The author regards this assumption as one which will prove fruitful in future research on problems of family organization, socialization processes, and related areas.

Positing achievement of higher status as a primary family group goal contains at least one important implication for the authority of fathers within families of different statuses; it follows that fathers in lower status families wield less influence in the family group. This implication rests first on the assumption that group members achieve status within their group according to their contribution to advancing the group toward its goals; those members who have the requisite skills or characteristics to achieve group goals will have more influence and prestige within the group. For example, boys' teams usually name their best player as captain.

The principle that influence in a group is related to members' varying contributions to group success suggests that fathers of lower status families are less influential; for the low status of the family itself implies that the father, who is primarily charged with the role of breadwinner, has not contributed to his family's achievement of group goals. To the extent that his family's low status is considered merely a temporary stage of their progress on up in the status system, a father's position will be strengthened. But probably most lower status families do not perceive themselves on the way up, and probably the father must carry the major burden for the failure of his family to achieve its goal. Indeed, it may be that achievement of upward mobility was never regarded as a realistic goal by a lower status man and his wife from the day of their marriage; but this condition similarly weakens the man's potential authority as a breadwinner.

Other factors related to the family group goal also tend to dissipate a father's influence in his family. If his wife is working, for example, she may be making as great a contribution to the family group goal as he and may command as much authority as he on that account. Further, if a man works in a strongly unionized industry, as the overwhelming majority of Flint fathers do, then the achievement of upward mobility, in terms of higher wages at least,

is largely out of his hands and is the responsibility of union executives. So there is reason to expect that, in general, fathers in lower status families are less influential members of their family
groups. This expectation runs counter to the image of the working
man as the burly lord of his household while the white collar man
shares if not concedes decision-making to his wife; but nevertheless,
it is the expectation derived from principles of group dynamics.

Several investigations in fact confirm this expectation. Gold
and Slater (1958) found that husbands who hold white collar jobs
have more influence over family decisions than husbands in blue
collar jobs. Furthermore, they found that wives were more influential in those situations where they could contribute to the achievement of upward mobility by working. U. Bronfenbrenner (*op. cit.*)
found that mothers in his sample were more influential in lower
status families. In her study of *The Unemployed Man and His Family* during the economic depression of the 1930's, M. Komarovsky
(1940) found that unemployment had the effect of weakening a man's
authority in his family. Moreover, Komarovsky found that unemployment especially weakened the authority of fathers over their adolescent sons, largely because of their failure as providers.

It seems reasonable to assume that a boy will be more attracted to his father if he regards his father as a success and if
his father is an influential member of his family. Both of these related factors make the father a figure more worthy of emulation.
Then the attraction which they generate may provide a basis for a
father's control over his boy.

Other Factors in Family Attractiveness

Another element of the father-son relationship is the technique
a father uses to discipline his boy when he misbehaves. A father
may, for example, spank or slap his son, take away a privilege or
dock him his allowance, reason with him, or perhaps do nothing at
all. The type of discipline a father employs may have some effect
on the father's attractiveness to his son, and it may also serve as
a lesson to the boy on how he should behave when he himself is
angry at someone.

Another characteristic of his family which may affect a boy's
attraction to it is whether or not his mother works. It is reasonable to assume that working mothers are generally less able to provide sons with the care and companionship, as well as the supervision which full-time mothers can. Kvaraceus (1945), and the

Gluecks (1950) are among those researchers who have found more mothers of delinquents employed than mothers of non-delinquents. But one doubtful aspect of the findings pertaining to employment of mothers in relation to delinquency is that adequate control for social status has not been applied.   It may be that employment is more prevalent among delinquents' mothers because it is more prevalent among mothers in the lower strata, where most delinquency occurs; so employment of mothers might itself have no functional relationship at all to delinquency.   It can be argued, for example, that the employment of the mother usually brings a second income into a home and helps to counteract delinquency by ameliorating some of the disadvantages of lower status.   The set of interviews presented in Chapter IV provide an illustration of this: the income of Phil's mother probably made it possible for this non-delinquent's family to live in an above-average neighborhood out of the reach of the father's income alone.   Presumably, his mother's income will also make it possible for Phil to continue his education after high school.   On the other hand, research has been cited which demonstrates that the employment of wives shapes the kind of authority relations with their husbands which may encourage delinquency among their sons.   The phenomenon of the relationship between employment of mothers and the delinquency of their sons needs more investigation.   The data bearing on it presented in this chapter suggest a new point of view.

Data will also be examined which bear on the findings often reported in the literature (c.f., Kvaraceus, *op. cit.*; Glueck and Glueck, *op. cit.*) that delinquents more frequently come from broken homes than do non-delinquents.

Consideration of various characteristics of families suggests that lower status families are less attractive to and consequently are less able to control their sons.   This may help to explain why lower status boys are more likely to become delinquent.   It is also possible that the unattractive features of lower status families exist, albeit less frequently, among higher status families and help to account in part for what higher status delinquency occurs.   The remainder of this chapter consists of the presentation and discussion of data relating to processes by which social status is linked to delinquency through its effect on the social control potential of boys' families.

Family Attractiveness, Control, and Delinquency

There are several indications that repeated delinquents were less attracted to their families than were their non-delinquent controls.

One measure of attraction is a boy's participation in any sort of activity with his parents. When boys were asked what sorts of things they did with their parents, more repeated delinquents replied, in effect, "nothing." The data in Tables 17 and 18 summarize the findings for participation with fathers and mothers respectively. About three-fourths of the boys interviewed were able to name something they did with their parents, like hunting, washing the car, or going to sports events with their fathers; playing cards, washing dishes, or going shopping with their mothers; and often watching television with both. While the number of pairs which differed on this variable is relatively few, only about a third of the sample, the repeated delinquents significantly more often reported no participation with their parents. The trend is consistent at all social status levels. The way the questions on this subject were put to the boys, it is not possible to learn much about the intensity or quality of the parent-child interaction during their time together, but perhaps the relationships among delinquents and their parents were also less warm. For example, among the repeated delinquents who are included with those who do something with their fathers are three for whom the activity is fighting and arguing.

Table 17

Repeated delinquents, especially in the skilled worker stratum, less often report doing things with their fathers than do non-delinquents.

Question 55: What sorts of things do you usually do with your father ?

		Repeated Delinquents	Non-Delinquents
WHITE COLLAR	Something	80%	80%
	Nothing	20%	5%
	No father	(N=20) 0%	15% (N=20)
SKILLED	Something	63%	85%
	Nothing	30%	15%
	No father	(27) 7%	0% (27)
UNSKILLED	Something	65%	89%
	Nothing	19%	11%
	No father	(46) 15%	0% (46)
TOTAL	Something	67%	80%
	Nothing	23%	11%
	No father	(93) 10%	3% (93)

Sign test summary (something vs. nothing): unequal pairs = 31%; p = .02

Table 18

Compared to non-delinquents, repeated delinquents less often report doing things with their mothers.

Question 56: What sorts of things do you usually do with your mother ?

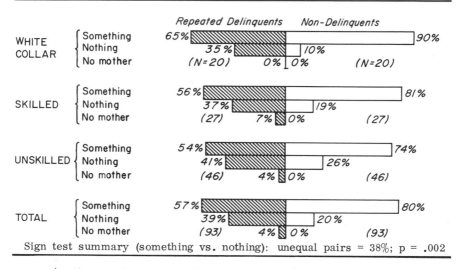

Sign test summary (something vs. nothing): unequal pairs = 38%; p = .002

Another indicator of the attraction of a boy to his family is
the extent to which he seeks his parents' help when he has personal problems. Table 19 demonstrates that fewer repeated delinquents felt they could talk about personal problems with adults,
mostly their parents, but were more likely to seek help from peers
or no one. Among white collar boys, this measure of attraction
shows little difference between filial attitudes of delinquents and non-
delinquents.

Data from other studies support the general picture here that
delinquents are less attracted to their family group. In the course
of the Gluecks' study (*op. cit.*), a psychiatrist judged that fewer of
the institutionalized delinquents than matched non-delinquents exhibited strong emotional ties to either parent, particularly to their fathers. Bandura and Walters (*op. cit.*) found that boys on probation
were less likely to seek help from their parents or spend time with
them, compared to matched non-delinquents. Moreover, Bandura's
and Walter's data revealed greater differences in these aspects of
attraction to fathers.

The data of the present study suggest that weaker attractions
may have the hypothesized implications for social control. Repeated

Table 19

Fewer repeated delinquents than non-delinquents feel they can take their personal problems to adults; they would more likely go to a peer or to no one.

Question 48: If you had some personal problem you wanted to talk about with someone, who do you feel you could talk with? Whom would you most likely go to?

		Repeated Delinquents	Non-Delinquents
WHITE COLLAR	Parents	80%	75%
	Sibs	10%	15%
	Adults	0%	10%
	Friends	10%	0%
	No one	(N=20) 0%	0% (N=20)
SKILLED	Parents	56%	81%
	Sibs	15%	7%
	Adults	5%	7%
	Friends	11%	4%
	No one	(27) 7%	0% (27)
UNSKILLED	Parents	50%	76%
	Sibs	15%	7%
	Adults	13%	7%
	Friends	13%	9%
	No one	(46) 9%	2% (46)
TOTAL	Parents	58%	77%
	Sibs	11%	8%
	Adults	9%	8%
	Friends	12%	5%
	No one	(93) 8%	2% (93)

Sign test summary (adults vs. peers or no one):
unequal pairs = 43%; p = .004 (1t)

delinquents seem to have accepted less strongly their parents' standards of behavior. As Table 20 indicates, the delinquent boys reported less agreement with their fathers and with their mothers about how they should behave. The differences are consistent and reliably large at the three social status levels.

It has been suggested that the father-son relationship is the more important one in the control of the child. Responses by parents themselves concerning the one aspect of direct control explored in this research indicate that the father's loss of control over his son may be more crucial to the boy becoming delinquent. Parents were asked about their influence over their sons' choice of friends. White collar and skilled mothers of delinquents and non-delinquents did not differ in estimates of their influence in this regard. But,

Table 20

Repeated delinquents report less agreement with their parents about standards for their behavior than non-delinquents do.

Question 44: When you think of how you should do things or what you ought to do-do you feel that you and ......

☐ *Non-Delinquents (N=93)*   ▨ *Repeated Delinquents (N=93)*

.... your **father** agree ? ....your **mother** agree?

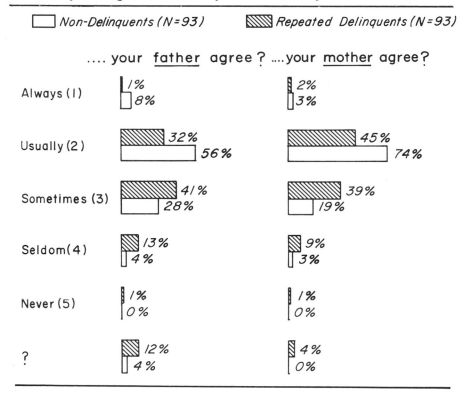

	White Collar		Skilled		Unskilled		Total			White Collar		Skilled		Unskilled		Total	
	Repeat-ers	Non-del.	Repeat-ers	Non-del.	Repeat-ers	Non-del.	Repeat-ers	Non-del.		Repeat-ers	Non-del.	Repeat-ers	Non-del.	Repeat-ers	Non-del.	Repeat-ers	Non-del.
Mean	2.6	2.2	3.0	2.3	2.8	2.4	2.8	2.3	Mean	2.6	2.3	2.8	2.3	2.5	2.2	2.6	2.2
N	16		24		38		78		N	20		24		45		89	
t	2.2		3.6		2.0		4.1		t	1.4		2.5		2.3		3.6	
p	<.01		<.003		<.03		<.0003		p	<.05		<.005		<.01		<.0003	

as Table 21 demonstrates, white collar and unskilled fathers differed considerably; the fathers of repeated delinquents felt they had less influence over their sons than did the other fathers. The data from skilled fathers tended unreliably in the other direction.

Table 21

Compared to the fathers of non-delinquents, the fathers of repeated delinquents feel they have less influence over their sons'
choices of friends; there is no difference among mothers.

Question 47 (parents): How much influence would you say you have in your son's selection of friends?

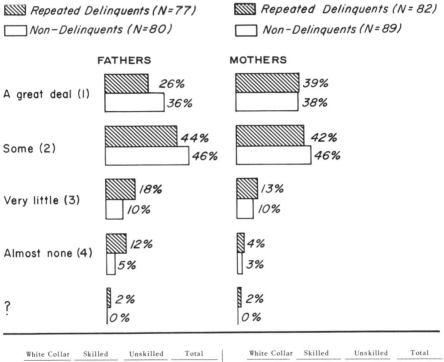

	White Collar		Skilled		Unskilled		Total			White Collar		Skilled		Unskilled		Total	
	Repeat- ers	Non- del.	Repeat- ers	Non- del.	Repeat- ers	Non- del.	Repeat- ers	Non- del.		Repeat- ers	Non- del.	Repeat- ers	Non- del.	Repeat- ers	Non- del.	Repeat- ers	Non- del.
Mean	2.2	1.7	1.9	2.0	2.3	1.8	2.1	1.9	Mean	1.7	1.9	1.8	1.9	2.0	1.6	1.84	1.76
N	14		20		32		66		N	17		20		38		75	
t	1.5		0.8		1.9		1.9		t	0.8		0.7		1.9		0.6	
p	<.05		NR		<.03		<.03		p	NR		NR		<.03		NR	

Perhaps the decision about a boy's choice of friends is unique
in respect to these findings about the influence of parents, and other
areas of control would not have duplicated these results. Unfortunately this was the only kind of direct influence investigated here,
and other studies do not add more information. Neither is it possible at this time to determine how representative is the choice of
friends among the decisions boys make. This decision is probably
not an unimportant one, however, since about three-fourths of the

fathers and mothers interviewed said they tried to influence their sons' choices of friends.   Eighty per cent of the fathers of repeated delinquents, who seemed to have the least effect, tried to exert some influence on this decision, compared to 58 per cent of the non-delinquents' fathers.

Sources of Attraction to Fathers

It has been shown that repeated delinquents are less likely to be attracted to their parents than non-delinquents.   In light of the possible primacy for social control of boys' attractions to their fathers, a more intensive investigation was made of father-son relationships in hopes of isolating some of their determinants.   It has been suggested that one of the direct or indirect factors affecting boys' attractions to their fathers is their fathers' role as provider for the family.   Not infrequently the breadwinner role factor was clearly present in boys' choices of adult models.   One boy said, "I want to be like my dad . . . He's doing OK, making a go of it . . ." Another youngster aspired to be "like the man who came in one of our classes and talked about architecture.   He was an architect. I'd like to be like him 'cause he said if he had it all to do over again, he would do the same thing."   One of the repeated delinquents had this to say about an adult model, "I want to be like Mr. F____. He's a detective—that's what I want to be."   The most frequent reason given by boys who chose adults as models had to do with the occupational roles the adults filled.   Often these occupations appeared again in boys' own occupational aspirations.

When boys were asked directly, "When you're older, who do you want to be like?" only about a fourth named their fathers.   The data indicate that on this measure of attraction to father, repeated delinquents and non-delinquents did not differ reliably.   However, results were quite different when the boys were asked to indicate their agreement to the check-list item, "When I become an adult, I'd like to be the kind of person my father is."   In a situation where they were marking a pencil-and-paper questionnaire form with no one to react immediately to their responses, and faced with no alternative but their fathers, repeated delinquents were less likely to accept their fathers as models than were non-delinquents.   The data are presented in Table 22, and although the complete breakdown is not included, the finding is the same for boys at each social status level.   Table 22 shows that most boys, delinquent and non-delinquent, agreed with the statement, but fewer delinquents agreed, and those who did tended to agree less strongly.   The Gluecks (op. cit.) similarly report that institutionalized delinquents less often emulated their fathers compared to non-delinquents.

Table 22

Fewer repeated delinquents than non-delinquents regard their fathers as adult models.

Question 20c (questionnaire): When I'm an adult I'd like to be the kind of person my father is.

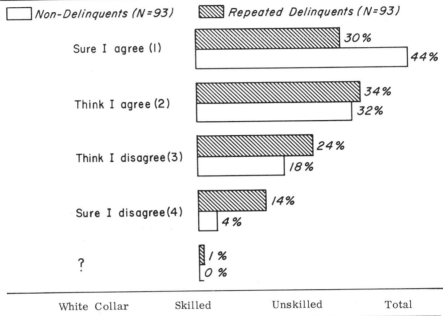

	White Collar		Skilled		Unskilled		Total	
	Repeat-ers	Non-del.	Repeat-ers	Non-del.	Repeat-ers	Non-del.	Repeat-ers	Non-del.
Mean	1.9	1.7	2.2	1.8	2.5	1.9	2.3	1.8
N	19		25		43		87	
t	0.8		1.5		2.8		3.2	
p	NR		<.05		<.003		<.003	

It has been suggested that one criterion by which boys accept or reject their fathers as adult models is their fathers' occupational success. Table 23 demonstrates that the more prestigeful a father's occupation, the more his son was likely to be sure he wanted to be like his father, although this relationship does not reach the level of reliability selected for this study. Data on non-delinquents only have been presented in this analysis because the non-delinquents studied are probably more representative of boys in general than are the matched repeated delinquents. The data on the latter group revealed the same relationship, however.

Data gathered among mental patients by J. K. Myers and B. H. Roberts (1959) support the present findings. These authors concluded:

> Since class V (the lowest class) parents could provide little economic security, most patients regarded them as failures. Patients could not develop much respect for parents who had difficulty providing them with even the minimal requirements of food, shelter and clothing, let alone any extras which most children take for granted. . . . Lacking respect for their parents, the patients rarely wanted to model themselves after them [1959, pp. 175-176].

While Myers' and Roberts' data refer to "parents who had difficulty providing . . . even the minimal requirements of food, shelter and clothing," the phenomenon they demonstrate is apparently not limited to destitute families. More direct confirmation for the somewhat unreliable relationships in Table 23 between boys' choice of father as an adult model and his social status can be found in a national study of Boys Club members (Scagnelli, 1960). Fourteen-to-18-year-old boys were asked, "When you are older, who do you want to be like?" and "father" was nominated by 35 per cent of the boys in the highest social status category, 29 per cent of those in the middle, and 19 per cent of those in the lowest. All of these data imply that youngsters become well aware of the American image of "the successful man" and compare their fathers to it. Fathers in blue collar occupations are often found wanting. Men with clean jobs and good prospects find it easier to win the respect of their sons and the control which follows upon it.

Summary

So data presented thus far suggest the following generalizations: first, that boys' attractions to their fathers are based in part upon their images of their fathers in the world of occupations; second, that perhaps on this account, lower status fathers are less attractive to their sons; third, that repeated delinquents are less attracted to both their parents; and fourth, that repeated delinquents less often accept their parents, especially their fathers' standards of behavior. Before the relationship between attraction and social control is pursued any further, another basis for a boy's attraction to his father is explored.

Table 23

The more prestigeful his father's occupation, the more likely a
son will be sure he wants to be like his father when he becomes
an adult (non-delinquent data only).

Question 20c (questionnaire): When I become an adult, I'd like to
be the kind of person my father is.

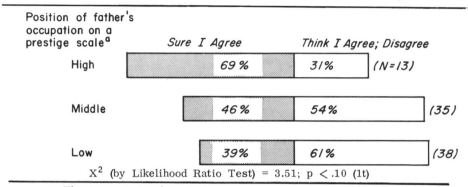

Position of father's occupation on a prestige scale[a]	Sure I Agree	Think I Agree; Disagree	
High	69 %	31%	(N=13)
Middle	46%	54%	(35)
Low	39%	61%	(38)

X^2 (by Likelihood Ratio Test) = 3.51; $p < .10$ (1t)

a. The Warner, Meeker, Eels scale is trichotomized so that the highest category includes professionals, managers, and proprietors of medium and
large-sized business, and upper white collar salesmen and executives; the
middle category includes owners of small businesses, lower white collar
salesmen and clerical workers, foremen, craftsmen, and skilled workers; the
lowest category includes semi-skilled and unskilled workers.

Parental Power and Attraction

It has been proposed that the more influence a father has in
his family group, the more attractive he is to his son. It has been
further proposed that a father's influence in relation to his wife depends in part upon his success as a breadwinner. One way of looking at the husband-wife power relationship is to suppose that wives
as well as sons find higher status husbands more admirable and are
more prone to submit to his authority. This kind of individual attitude process may lie behind the general fact of group life that
members who advance group goals tend to be more influential in
making group decisions.

Data from the present study confirm earlier findings about
influence in the family group; men holding white collar jobs were
the more influential fathers according to their sons, their wives,
and themselves (see Table 24). Skilled workers and unskilled workers did not differ in family power, perhaps because upward mobility
for almost all the Flint men in these strata depended not so much

on their own efforts but on the efforts of the United Auto Workers. These findings are important to the question of social status links to social control over boys if it can be shown that fathers' power positions in their families do in fact relate to their attractiveness to their sons.

Table 24

White collar fathers make more of the decisions in their families than do skilled or unskilled worker fathers, according to the boys, mothers, and fathers in the non-delinquent sample.

Question 4: 1-9 (questionnaire) (parents, Questions 54a-i): Who would have the final say if (your father and mother) (you and your spouse) disagreed about—where to go for vacation? which doctor to call? the wife working? how much money to spend on food for the family? giving son permission? which house or apartment to move to? buying life insurance? husband changing his job?

	Means, Parental Power Indices					
	Boys' Responses		Mothers' Responses		Fathers' Responses	
	Pct.	N	Pct.	N	Pct.	N
White collar	26.4[a]	18	26.8	16	26.4	10
Skilled	24.0	27	25.2	23	24.2	23
Unskilled	24.5	42	25.2	38	24.4	33
N............	60		43		54	
t	2.0		1.3		1.6	
p...........	<.03		<.06		<.05	

a. Mother always decides: score = 8
Equal power: score = 24
Father always decides: score = 40

In order to investigate the relationship between power position and fathers' attractiveness, it was necessary to decide just who was to be the judge of a father's power position; for while men, women, and boys yielded the same results pertaining to power and social class, they were by no means in complete agreement on power ratings. The correlations in Table A-6 reveal that the perceptions of family members were with one exception reliably related to one another, but the relationships were moderate at best. It is also worth noting now that correlations in delinquents' families (first column) are consistently lower than those in non-delinquents' families (fourth column); this is discussed later.   A decision was made to use boys' ratings of power to test the relationship between fathers' power positions and boys' attractions, since the boys' perceptions of the situation were the ultimate determinants of their attitudes.

Family power ratings of boys who agreed they'd like to grow up to be like their fathers were compared to the ratings of boys who disagreed.   The data, summarized in Table 25, indicate that repeated delinquents who agreed they would like to become adults like their fathers tended to report their fathers as having more power in their families, compared to repeated delinquents who reject their fathers as models.   The data are not so clear-cut among non-delinquents, however: among white collar non-delinquents, the difference between boys who accept and reject their fathers is reliably in the opposite direction; among skilled non-delinquents, unreliably in the expected

Table 25

Repeated delinquents who accept their fathers as models rate them higher in parental power than do boys who reject them; the findings are mixed among non-delinquents.

	Mean Score: Agree	N	Mean Score: Dis- agree	N	t	p
Repeated Delinquents						
White collar	26.1	14	23.2	5	1.65	<.05
Skilled	27.1	15	24.6	9	1.62	<.05
Unskilled	25.1	25	21.3	17	2.30	<.01
Total	25.9	54	22.6	31	3.27	<.003
Non-Delinquents						
White collar	26.1	15	28.3	3	1.41	<.05
Skilled	24.4	21	22.2	5	1. 06	<.10
Unskilled	24.8	30	23.3	11	1.47	<.05
Total	25.0	66	23.8	19	.92	<.10

direction; and among unskilled non-delinquents, reliably in the expected direction. Because the non-delinquents are probably more representative of boys generally than are the repeated delinquents, their responses should be weighted more heavily in testing the hypothesis relating parental power and attractiveness of fathers. These data then do not strongly support the hypothesis.

Norm Support by Models and Delinquency

It was proposed earlier that attraction to persons or groups which do not support the usual social norms do not lead to boys accepting these norms but instead weakens normative control. For example, if a boy's adult model is a gangster, the boy is likely to accept gangster standards of behavior rather than lawful standards. According to this point of view, repeated delinquents are likely to have models who are less ardent norm-supporters than the models for non-delinquents. L. E. Hewitt and R. L. Jenkins (*op. cit.*) isolated a type of delinquent who seemed to fit this pattern and called him "the socialized delinquent"; this type is socialized by, or has accepted the norms of, delinquent groups or models.

One indication that this phenomenon occurs among delinquents in the present study comes from data on boys' choices of whom they would "rather be like as a person, Pat Boone or Elvis Presley?" It was supposed that Presley is a model perceived as more tolerant of delinquent behavior than Boone, for reasons already discussed in Chapter IV; boys who chose Presley did in fact report him to be more tolerant of behavior like eating a stolen pie than did boys who chose Boone. Table 26 demonstrates that few boys actually chose Presley as a model, but considering only those boys who made a choice, more delinquents than non-delinquents were among those few. Of course, this finding has little to do with Presley's actual opinions, or Boone's, for that matter. It may be that boys adopt their own attitudes toward delinquent behavior first, then choose models who they believe share them. On the other hand, a model may be chosen first, and he may help shape the attitudes of his followers.

After boys selected a model, they were asked what their model would think about each of a series of three delinquent acts: breaking into a school cafeteria and eating a pie; throwing over school desks and wastebaskets; and seriously damaging and defacing school property. An approval index was constructed simply by assigning each response a score of 1 for complete approval and a score of 5 for rigorous disapproval. Average approval scores are presented in Table 27. It is apparent that all the boys felt their models would

Table 26

Given a choice between Pat Boone and Elvis Presley, more repeated delinquents than non-delinquents want to be like Presley.

Question 40: Who would you rather be like as a person, Pat Boone or Elvis Presley?

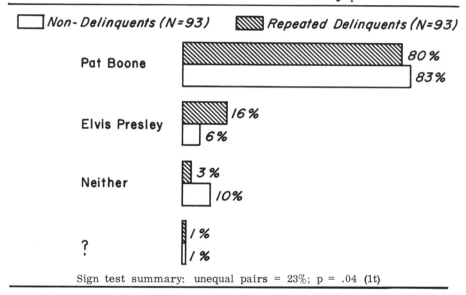

☐ Non-Delinquents (N=93)   ▨ Repeated Delinquents (N=93)

Pat Boone   80%
                   83%

Elvis Presley   16%
                    6%

Neither   3%
                   10%

?   1%
                    1%

Sign test summary: unequal pairs = 23%; p = .04 (1t)

largely disapprove of these behaviors.   But the degree of disapproval varied; more of the delinquents thought that their models
would regard at least one of these acts as "wild but not serious."
While the mean scores do not differ much, all the scores were so
tightly packed at the disapproval end of the scale that even the slight
reduction in average disapproval noted by the repeated delinquents
is reliably different from the average non-delinquent score.   Now
this difference among the boys might be due simply to perceptual
distortion on the part of the repeated delinquents.   What is striking,
however, is that parents' actual reactions to the same set of delinquent acts also showed reliable differences paralleling the findings
among the boys.   While the parents of repeated delinquents disapproved of the delinquencies, they did not as consistently hold the
line as did the parents of non-delinquents.

Although it seems that more of the parents of repeated delinquents did not so vigorously support the norms of their community,
interpretation of these data must be made cautiously.   It may be

Table 27

Repeated delinquents perceive their chosen models to be less disapproving of delinquent acts than non-delinquents do; the parents of repeated delinquents do in fact express less disapproval of these acts than do non-delinquents' parents.

Question 39: Would (boy's model) (you) think each of these acts was (1) OK, (2) wild but not serious, (3) getting serious, or (4) very serious: (a) breaking into the school cafeteria at night with some friends and eating a pie? (b) breaking into school at night with some friends and throwing over wastebaskets and desks? (c) breaking into school at night with some friends and breaking up desks and tables and smearing paint on the walls?

	Boys' Responses		Mothers' Responses		Fathers' Responses	
	Repeaters	Non-del.	Repeaters	Non-del.	Repeaters	Non-del.
Mean	10.6[a]	11.2	10.9	11.2	11.1	11.7
N	84		77		68	
t	2.9		2.0		3.5	
p	<.003		<.01		<.0003	

a. Maximum approval = 3.00
   Maximum disapproval = 12.00

that the parents of delinquents did not feel this way about these delinquent behaviors *before* their sons became delinquent but became more elastic about norms after their sons began to snap them. Perhaps in comparison to what their sons had actually done, the delinquents' parents could regard stealing a pie as merely "wild" or "getting serious"; and perhaps some minimizing and softening of their son's misdeeds was involved in their greater tolerance. If this was the case, it would not be accurate to conclude that the parents' weaker disapproval weakened controls over their sons; rather, weakened controls and consequent delinquency probably modulated their disapproval. It was possible to make one test to compare the adequacy of these two explanations: data were analyzed to see if repeated delinquents who said their parents were not so disapproving of delinquent behaviors actually had less disapproving parents. If boys' perceptions of their parents' attitudes toward delinquent behaviors did not vary directly with their parents' reported attitudes, then the latter was probably not shaping the former. Analysis of the data demonstrated that the repeated delinquent boys who perceived their parents to support norms less strongly were as often the sons of parents who rigidly held the line against delinquent behaviors as the sons of those who were less disapproving. These data favor the explanation that some parents respond to their sons' delinquency by lowering their behavior standards. The boys' choices of models seem related in part to their own sometimes incorrect estimates of their models' attitudes toward delinquency.

Discipline Techniques

An investigation was also made of the techniques of discipline employed by parents of delinquents and non-delinquents, with the idea that some types of discipline would weaken the attractiveness of the parent more than others would. It seems intuitively that being struck or deprived of something is more likely to alienate a boy from his parents than if he were reasoned with. A check was made on this intuition by comparing non-delinquent boys whose fathers reported they used physical punishment or deprivation with boys whose fathers preferred to reason, talk, or do nothing when their sons misbehaved. Less than one-fourth of the boys who were physically punished or deprived said they took their personal problems to their fathers; over half of the boys who were reasoned with or left alone sought their fathers' help. The data are summarized in Table 28. The importance of boys' relationships with their fathers is emphasized by the fact, demonstrated in Table 28, that mothers' discipline techniques did not seem to have the alienating effects of fathers'. Indeed, maternal discipline techniques of repeated delinquents seem to have the exact opposite effect: half of the 30 repeated delinquents whose mothers struck them or deprived them took their personal problems to their mothers; only 29 per cent of the 51 whose mothers reasoned or talked with them sought their mothers' help, while the rest looked elsewhere.

The expectation prompted by the relationship between fathers' discipline techniques and parental attractiveness is confirmed by an analysis of data summarized in Table 29, more parents of the repeated delinquents than of non-delinquents employ physical punishment and deprivation, differences among fathers being more striking. "I don't get punished," said one non-delinquent boy, "we talk it out instead"; his father reported, "I talk to him and I try to reason with him. I never have punished him." More characteristic of discipline applied to delinquent boys is described by one of them: ". . . my father beats me . . ."; his father agreed, "I usually whip him good." Findings by the Gluecks (op. cit.) on techniques of discipline are similar.

Table 28

Non-delinquent boys are more likely to take their personal problems to fathers who reason with them or do nothing when they misbehave than to fathers who use physical punishment or deprivation: mothers' discipline techniques do not have this effect consistently.

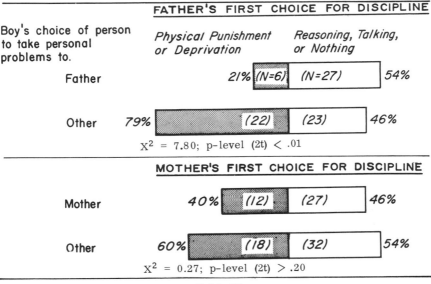

FATHER'S FIRST CHOICE FOR DISCIPLINE

Boy's choice of person to take personal problems to.	Physical Punishment or Deprivation	Reasoning, Talking, or Nothing	
Father	21% (N=6)	(N=27)	54%
Other	79% (22)	(23)	46%

$X^2 = 7.80$; p-level (2t) $< .01$

MOTHER'S FIRST CHOICE FOR DISCIPLINE

	Physical Punishment or Deprivation	Reasoning, Talking, or Nothing	
Mother	40% (12)	(27)	46%
Other	60% (18)	(32)	54%

$X^2 = 0.27$; p-level (2t) $> .20$

Table 29

More fathers of repeated delinquents than of non-delinquents usually punish their sons' misbehaviors physically or by depriving them of some privileges; differences in discipline by mothers tend in the same direction.

Question 37 (parents): Thinking of the times when (your son) has mis-behaved in the past one or two years, what have you usu-ally done about it?

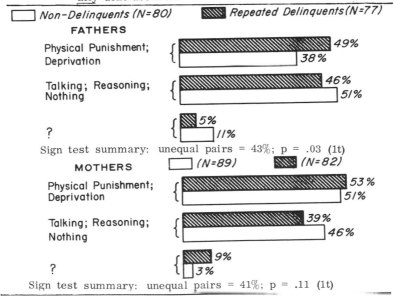

☐ Non-Delinquents (N=80)   ▨ Repeated Delinquents (N=77)

FATHERS

Physical Punishment; Deprivation
49%
38%

Talking; Reasoning; Nothing
46%
51%

?
5%
11%

Sign test summary: unequal pairs = 43%; p = .03 (1t)

MOTHERS   ☐ (N=89)   ▨ (N=82)

Physical Punishment; Deprivation
53%
51%

Talking; Reasoning; Nothing
39%
46%

?
9%
3%

Sign test summary: unequal pairs = 41%; p = .11 (1t)

Boys and their parents did not always agree about the discipline practices used in their families. One non-delinquent reported that, when he misbehaved, "Either I stay in or get a whipping." His father's report differed: "I try to talk to him and show him where he was wrong. I never clobber him." And his mother neatly contributed a compromise report: "Usually we talk and try to reason with him. We might take away a privilege by making him go to bed a half hour or so earlier or not allow him out of the yard. We don't strike him now. We might have done it when he was younger." It was supposed that the reports of delinquent boys might be distorted in the direction of the findings expected, but that fathers' reports, if distorted, would conceal physical punishment and deprivation. So to be on the safe side, fathers' reports were used, with the expected results nevertheless emerging, as Tables 28 and 29 have shown.

Some further discussion is demanded by an issue concerning disciplinary techniques. The hypothesis which directed the research on discipline practices was derived from the more general theory of attraction and social control and posits that physical punishment and deprivation permit delinquency by weakening attractions. The reverse of this process seems equally conceivable, however; that is, delinquent behavior may demand physical punishment and deprivations. Perhaps the parents of repeated delinquents had abandoned techniques of reasoning, talking, and doing nothing because they plainly did not work. Some data were collected during the first year of the Flint Youth Study which support one causal direction rather than the other (Gold, 1958). Parents of school behavior problems and parents of notably well-behaved school boys were asked not only about their current practices but also about how they had dealt with their sons' misbehaviors as they were growing up from early childhood. It was clear that more parents of school behavior problems had been employing physical punishment and deprivation all along, even before they had noticed that their sons were any more troublesome than the average boy. These data suggest that the process which produced the association of physical punishment and deprivation with delinquency begins with discipline techniques more often than with the nature or persistence of boys' misbehaviors.

Before leaving the subject of discipline techniques, it is important to recognize a link they may provide between social status and delinquency. It has been suggested that physical punishment and deprivation are associated with delinquency. Furthermore, Miller and Swanson (1958) gathered data showing that they are more often employed by working-class than by middle-class parents. The present data on techniques of discipline among the parents of non-delinquents show similar trends from one status level to the next, but these trends are unreliable.   Miller's and Swanson's data are, however, to be trusted more on this issue because they were gathered from a much larger and more representative sample.   If lower status boys are in fact more often punished for misbehavior in ways which would make their parents, especially their fathers, less attractive to them and hence less controlling, then they are more likely to commit delinquent acts when sufficiently provoked.   Type of punishment becomes, in this light, a variable among the forces of social control which may direct boys to delinquent outlets for their feelings and delinquent solutions for their problems.

Working Mothers

The next variable in family attractiveness to be considered is the employment of the mother.   It has been proposed that, since working mothers cannot provide the care and companionship which unemployed mothers can, their employment tends to weaken their sons' attraction to their families.   Previous research has been cited which demonstrates that delinquents more often have working mothers, but it was pointed out that the factor of social status was not so well controlled in these studies and may have been the effective variable.

Table 30 presents the results of the analysis of data on working mothers at each social status level.   Only among white collar men's families did significantly more mothers of repeated delinquents work.   Indeed, the relationship is reversed among unskilled workers' families, although far short of reliability.   The trustworthiness of this finding is enhanced by the fact that it is a duplication of the finding about working mothers uncovered by the author in an unpublished analysis of earlier Flint Youth Study data.   The earlier research revealed that only among boys who lived in middle-class neighborhoods did school behavior problems more often have working mothers.   The Study's first year research design made another suggestive finding possible which the present design did not: only among high school boys, compared to elementary school boys, did behavior problem boys more often have working mothers.   This pattern of results suggests that the care, companionship, and supervision elements related to mothers' employment are not the important ones, otherwise they should have similar effects across age levels and social strata.   The data point rather to the element of choice on the part of mothers to work or not to work; for choice is less open to a mother in the working class, who often must work to supplement her husband's income, and to a mother of an elementary

Table 30

Working wives of white collar men are more likely to have repeated delinquent sons than are non-working wives; this is not
true in the other socio-economic categories.

Question 15(mothers): Do you do any part-time or full-time work for pay?

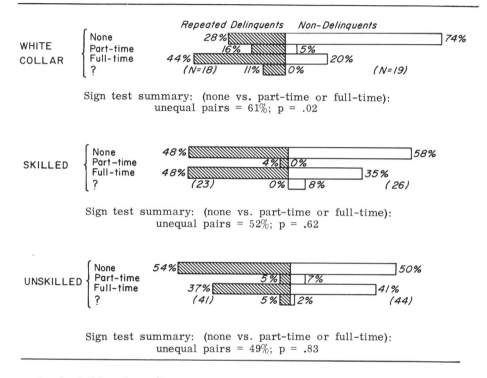

Sign test summary: (none vs. part-time or full-time):
unequal pairs = 61%; p = .02

Sign test summary: (none vs. part-time or full-time):
unequal pairs = 52%; p = .62

Sign test summary: (none vs. part-time or full-time):
unequal pairs = 49%; p = .83

school child, who often cannot work but must remain at home to
care for her younger children.   When a middle-class woman or the
mother of older children works, she may be expressing a feeling of
hers about the role of wife and mother; that is, a woman who chooses
to work when the choice is largely up to her may be indicating that
she does not get as much satisfaction out of her family role as a
woman who chooses not to work.

One may jump easily from this formulation of the psychology
of the working woman to the conclusion that working mothers, at
least those in higher social strata, more often have delinquent sons
because they neglect and perhaps even reject them.   But data collected by L. W. Hoffman (1961), a colleague at the Institute for Social Research, cast doubt on this conclusion.   She found that middle-

class working mothers were not neglectful or rejecting mothers, but to the contrary, were more indulgent of their children than most of the other mothers studied.   Hoffman's data suggest that many women who choose to work are ambivalent about their roles as wives and mothers, not decisively negative about them, and consequently they feel some guilt about choosing to work.   Perhaps to assuage their guilt, they indulge their children.   In such a roundabout way, the effect of the employment of mothers becomes a factor in the social control families may exert over their sons; but a relaxation of controls replaces the weakening of attractions as the underlying theoretical dynamic.

From the data presented here and from the interpretation which they and other data suggest, the factor of working mothers does not seem to help explain why lower status boys are more often delinquent.   It may, however, be more helpful in accounting for delinquency committed by higher status boys.

Broken Homes

The last summary of data presented in this chapter pertains to the factor of broken homes, which has been considered as another element affecting the social control potential of families.   Broken homes may imply either the absence of suitable models for boys or a history of parental discord which signals the absence of consistent standards for behavior.   Data were not collected which might sort out the processes through which broken homes and delinquency are associated.   It can be reported, however, that the present study confirms previous findings: repeated delinquents reliably more often came from broken homes.   There were too few broken homes, only three among white collar families, to establish a trend, so the results refer almost exclusively to blue collar families, especially to those of unskilled workers.   The larger proportion of broken homes among lower status families itself suggests that this factor may link delinquency to social status.   But the small number of broken homes and the relatively small proportion of matched pairs which differed in this respect imply that this factor is not a crucial link between social status and delinquency.

Summary

Two different measures of attraction to family demonstrate that repeated delinquents are less attracted than are non-delinquents: they share activities less with their parents and they take their personal problems to their parents less often. That their lower attraction to their families affects the amount of control their families have over them is suggested by the finding that repeated delinquents agree less with their parents about proper standards of behavior.

It appears that attraction and control in father-son relationships are more crucial to delinquent behavior than are mother-son relationships. While delinquent boys appear to have weak ties with their mothers as well, data on control over boys' companions suggest that differences in control of delinquent compared to non-delinquent boys is greater with regard to the father. The data further reveal two ways in which social status is related to attraction to father: the higher a father's status in his society, that is, the greater the prestige of his job, the more his son is likely to be attracted to him; and the more a father employs physical punishment and deprivation to discipline his son, practices more characteristic of lower than higher status fathers, the less attractive he will be to his son. Only among non-delinquent boys was fathers' power in their families clearly related to boys' attraction to their fathers, with greater power associated with greater attraction; the findings are ambiguous among delinquent boys. The data do indicate, however, that white collar fathers are more influential than are skilled and unskilled fathers.

Whatever models boys choose to emulate, it seems that repeated delinquents perceive their models as being less disapproving of delinquent behavior. The data suggest, however, that this is a consequence of perceptual distortion rather than a true reflection of the norm-support given by parents and other models.

Employment among mothers is related to delinquency only in the white collar category. This finding, taken along with results of some earlier studies, suggests that choosing to work when she need not is an index to a woman's feelings about the mother's role. Employment seems to be associated with guilt feelings and indulgence toward children and may consequently be related to delinquency as weakened controls.

Finally, data here confirm that delinquents are more likely to come from broken homes.

Chapter VII

OCCUPATIONAL FUTURES AS SOURCES OF PROVOCATIONS TO DELINQUENCY

This chapter describes an effort to expand in two ways on the theory advanced by A. K. Cohen in his book *Delinquent Boys*. This effort at expansion was prompted by two limitations of *Delinquent Boys*: first, the theory is stated there in a way which restricts it to explaining only lower-class, and not middle-class delinquency; and second, the work is mainly theoretical and draws only indirect support for its assumptions and assertions from the empirical findings of others. In this work, the theory that status problems lie back of delinquent behavior is made relevant to middle-class delinquency as well, and a direct empirical test of the theory is reported.

Occupational Futures and Delinquency: Theory

A brief review of the present theory and its hypotheses will orient the reader to the report of findings which follow. The status problems boys experience may be both sources of provocation to and of weakened social controls against delinquent behaviors. Boys may be provoked to break laws repeatedly and seriously in order to maintain the self-respect and the respect of others which they fear to lose when it becomes apparent they will not achieve the symbols of prestige their society prizes. Law-breaking maintains respect in at least two ways: it shows iconoclastic disdain for social criteria of prestige in ways like flaunting the sanctity of property by destroying it, and by seizing power illegitimately through violent defense of "turf" and assaults on persons; at the same time these behaviors gain boys the respect of their fellows. The reader may recall from Chapter IV that Jimmy's father seemed to feel these forces were acting upon his delinquent son: he thought Jimmy got into trouble with the police because "he thinks he's a big shot." Jimmy's mother agreed, explaining that Jimmy behaved badly because he wanted "to show off."

At the same time that status problems are provoking to delinquency, they also weaken social controls by making the community

151

and the future less attractive. So what if a boy gets a police record, what does he lose? He can't get a good job? He gets sent away? He won't get a good job anyway, and who wants to stay in this town! With little attractive to offer, the community has difficulty securing conforming behavior.

This theory of provocations and controls relevant to status and delinquency may be extended to middle-class boys in two ways. First, it may be that some middle-class boys find themselves in a situation more prevalent among their working-class peers; that is, they may perceive themselves for some reason unlikely to achieve status or even to maintain the status they now enjoy. On the other hand, control may be lost if these boys believe that their futures are assured no matter how they behave as adolescents.

At least two assumptions underlie the theory that status problems generate delinquent behavior. One is that for most boys, occupational future is an important factor in their lives during junior and senior high school, when juvenile delinquency occurs most frequently. Another is the assumption that most boys are striving for the same prestige symbols and gauge their success by comparing themselves to "all comers," regardless of differences in social status beginnings. If these assumptions are valid, then it would follow that status problems would more frequently be felt by lower status boys and would be potent enough to direct their behaviors.

The central hypothesis of the theory is that status problems are more often found among delinquents than among non-delinquents. So it became important for the purposes of this empirical study to determine what constitutes evidence for the presence of status problems. It seemed reasonable to assume a boy was demonstrating a status problem when his job aspirations were different from his job expectations. For example, if a boy told his interviewer that he hoped to become a doctor but then indicated that he expected to become a worker in an automobile factory, he was considered to have a status problem. That is, a discrepancy between occupational aspiration and expectation was the phenomenon focused upon.

This discrepancy was expected to occur in different directions for lower status and higher status boys. It was hypothesized that lower status repeated delinquents would have higher aspirations than expectations, compared to matched non-delinquents. But among higher status boys the repeated delinquents were expected to demonstrate smaller discrepancies than their non-delinquent controls and be more sure of getting the jobs they wanted. Data were also gathered which might help to discover the sources of the boys' aspirations and expectations, especially to throw some light on how parents might influence them.

In the course of analyzing and interpreting the data, however, it became apparent that the presence of a status problem could not usually be detected using discrepancies between occupational aspirations and expectations. Where such discrepancies may have existed, they seemed to give rise to feelings of personal failure on the part of the boys and to set in motion psychological processes which eradicated manifest evidence of discrepancies. It proved very interesting to trace the sources of feelings of personal failure and their relationship to the social status system and delinquency. As the data made the process-links more clear, so did the similarity between some of the causes of lower and higher status delinquency become more apparent.

The data pertaining to job futures and interpretations of their relevancy to delinquency make up the rest of this chapter. Data and interpretations have been organized primarily to present the resulting picture most clearly, so the retrospective quality of many of the interpretations is not obvious.

The Importance of Jobs to Boys

Occupational futures seem to be a rather important part of the psychological present for most boys, even for boys still in junior high school. The data in Table 31 show that about three-fourths of the boys replied spontaneously to a question about possible impending decisions in terms of jobs or further education. More than half reported that the job future had been on their minds "a great deal." Many parents said that they talk with their sons about the future. For example, in the sample set of interviews presented in Chapter IV, Phil's mother told her interviewer that she and Phil "discuss how the different professions would be." Jimmy's mother reported that her son talked with her about "what he wants to be when he grows up." As Table 32 indicates, there is a slight tendency for repeated delinquents to report that they think more often about future jobs, but the difference between them and their matched controls is not reliable.

Aspirations of Parents and The American Dream

The parents in this study often could not say what kind of jobs they would like their sons to have as adults. Most of the undecided fathers and mothers represented in the "not ascertained" (?) column of Table A-7 answered to the effect that "it's up to him." Of

Table 31

For most boys interviewed, both delinquent and not, to think about the future means to think about a job or career planning.

Question 18: What do you think are the things you will have to make up your mind about now or in the future ?

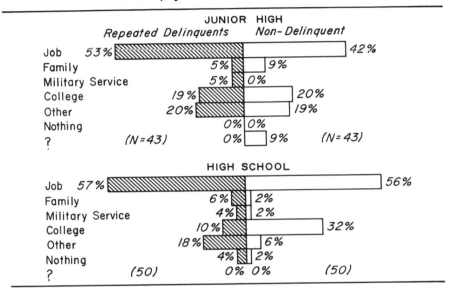

JUNIOR HIGH

Repeated Delinquents   *Non-Delinquent*

Job	53%	42%
Family	5%	9%
Military Service	5%	0%
College	19%	20%
Other	20%	19%
Nothing	0%	0%
?	(N=43) 0%	9% (N=43)

HIGH SCHOOL

Job	57%	56%
Family	6%	2%
Military Service	4%	2%
College	10%	32%
Other	18%	6%
Nothing	4%	2%
?	(50) 0%	0% (50)

Table 32

Most boys, both delinquent and not, report thinking a great deal about the kinds of jobs they will have as adults.

Question 24: How much would you say you've thought about what job you'll have when you're older?

	A Great Deal	Some	A Little	None	N
Junior high					
Repeated delinquents	67%	24%	5%	5%	43
Non-delinquents	51	35	12	2	43
High school					
Repeated delinquents	55	29	12	4	50
Non-delinquents	52	44	4	--	50

those who did state occupational aspiration levels, the great majority hoped their sons would enter the professions, as the percentages in the first column indicate. Moreover, there is reason to
believe that even those parents who said they were leaving it up to
their sons to set their own goals actually held high aspirations for
them which almost certainly must have been communicated. One
mother said, "I want my boy to do the things that would make him
happy. Of course, I hope he might be a minister or a dentist."
Another replied with some displeasure in her tone, "Let him be a
farmer as long as he wants it so bad. It's not what I'd choose."
Still another mother said, "I don't feel Mitchell will ever be a professional man. He is more mechanical minded, working with his
hands. As a mother I had high hopes he would be a doctor, lawyer,
or dentist. His grandfather is a lawyer, so I would naturally like
him to be a lawyer."

The data in Table A-7 indicate that white collar and unskilled
worker fathers of repeated delinquents do not have as high occupational aspirations for their sons as fathers of matched non-delinquents. This finding is reversed, but unreliably so, in the unskilled
category, and there are no reliable differences among the mothers
at all. It should also be noted in Table A-7 that in all six comparisons of parents of delinquents with parents of non-delinquents, a
larger proportion of the latter hope their sons will enter the top
three occupational categories. Parents of delinquents either have
lower or vague, uncodable aspirations for their sons.

Not only does it seem that many parents have high aspirations for their sons, but most of them also believe that whether or
not their sons achieve these aspirations depends upon the motivations and ability of the boys themselves, not upon the conditions of
their social status or other social influences. That is, most parents professed belief in The American Dream. Parents were asked
if they thought "all boys had an equal chance to get the jobs they
wanted." Some unqualifiedly answered, "Yes," and others said "No"
but mentioned only differences in effort and ability to account for
differences in opportunity; both of these kinds of responses are consistent with The American Dream. On the other hand, some parents cited "pull," social position, finances, and the like as responsible for differences in opportunity; these were taken as indications
of disbelief in The Dream.

Among believers, for example, is the non-delinquent's father
who said, "All they've got to do is to be interested enough to work
for it. That would depend on how bad they wanted it"; and the repeated delinquent's mother, who answered, "If they're determined

and set their mind and ambitions to it, I feel they have a pretty good chance. It may take them a while, but in our country, in America, they have a wonderful chance. It depends upon the individual." Other parents clearly showed disbelief: "No, I think politics have a lot to do with it, the people you know"; "All boys don't have equal chances. Some haven't the education others have. Financial reasons would make it necessary for some to go to work"; and "Financially, some people can't afford it. There are some smart boys who should be there, but they aren't because they don't have the chance."

A few parents responded in ways which made them difficult to categorize as believers or disbelievers in The American Dream, like the father who said, "Some don't have the ability or money that others do." Where any response seemed to indicate disbelief, the respondent was categorized as a disbeliever, as this last father was. Where the response was more ambiguous or clearly "I don't know," the respondent was considered uncertain.

Table 33 indicates that, even with pushing hedgers into the disbelievers category, most parents subscribe to The American Dream. Fathers of repeated delinquents did not respond significantly differently from the fathers of non-delinquents. On the other hand, mothers at all three status levels showed the same trend,

Table 33

Mothers of repeated delinquents are somewhat more likely to believe in The American Dream than are mothers of non-delinquents: there is no sizeable difference among fathers.

Question 35: Do you think all boys have an equal chance of getting the jobs they want ? Why do you say that ?

		FATHERS		MOTHERS	
		Repeated Delinquents	Non-Delinquents	Repeated Delinquents	Non-Delinquents
WHITE COLLAR	Does not believe in The American Dream	39%	19%	28%	53%
	Uncertain	0%	13%	6%	11%
	Believes in The American Dream	61% (N=18)	69% (N=16)	67% (N=18)	37% (N=19)
SKILLED	Does not believe in The American Dream	23%	33%	17%	38%
	Uncertain	23%	0%	4%	11%
	Believes in The American Dream	55% (22)	67% (24)	78% (23)	54% (26)
UNSKILLED	Does not believe in The American Dream	41%	45%	37%	45%
	Uncertain	11%	0%	10%	7%
	Believes in The American Dream	49% (37)	55% (40)	54% (41)	48% (44)
TOTAL	Does not believe in The American Dream	35%	36%	29%	45%
	Uncertain	12%	3%	7%	8%
	Believes in The American Dream	53% (77)	61% (80)	63% (82)	47% (89)

Sign test summary (believes vs. other):   Sign test summary (believes vs. other):
   unequal pairs = 51%; p = .31 (1t)   unequal pairs = 50%; p = .07 (1t)

Table 34

Compared to the parents of non-delinquents, parents of repeated delinquents do not believe their sons's chances are so good to get the kinds of jobs they would like to get.

Question 33: What do you think are (your son's) chances of getting that (kind of job you would like him to have)?

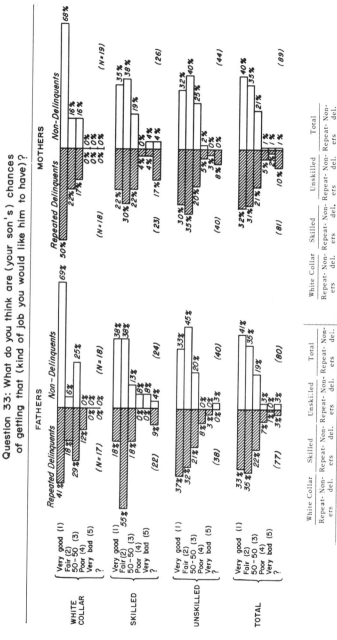

	White Collar		Skilled		Unskilled		Total	
	Repeat-ers	Non-del.	Repeat-ers	Non-del.	Repeat-ers	Non-del.	Repeat-ers	Non-del.
Mean	2.1	1.6	2.0	1.9	2.1	1.8	2.1	1.8
N	15		18		32		65	
t	1.2		0.2		1.3		1.7	
p	NR		NR		<.05		<.03	

	White Collar		Skilled		Unskilled		Total	
	Repeat-ers	Non-del.	Repeat-ers	Non-del.	Repeat-ers	Non-del.	Repeat-ers	Non-del.
Mean	1.7	1.6	2.3	2.0	2.2	1.9	2.1	1.8
N	16		17		37		70	
t	0.4		0.8		1.4		1.6	
p	NR		NR		<.05		<.05	

which is not quite statistically reliable in the total table: the mothers of repeated delinquents more often subscribed to The American Dream.

Just as parental aspirations for repeated delinquents seemed to be somewhat lower than aspirations for non-delinquents, so also did expectations differ. Parents were asked, "What do you think your son's chances are of getting the kind of job he wants?" The total figures in Table 34 indicate that expectations are lower among both fathers and mothers of repeated delinquents. These differences appear among parents in all social status categories.

Table 35

Parents of repeated delinquents believe their sons will need less education for their future jobs than do parents of non-delinquents.

Question 28: How much schooling do you think (your son) will really need to have for what he's likely to do when he's an adult?

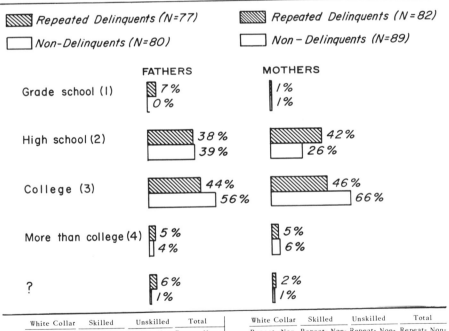

	White Collar		Skilled		Unskilled		Total			White Collar		Skilled		Unskilled		Total	
	Repeaters	Non-del.	Repeaters	Non-del.	Repeaters	Non-del.	Repeaters	Non-del.		Repeaters	Non-del.	Repeaters	Non-del.	Repeaters	Non-del.	Repeaters	Non-del.
Mean	2.6	2.8	2.5	2.5	2.4	2.6	2.5	2.6	Mean	1.8	1.8	2.5	3.0	2.5	2.7	2.6	2.8
N	14		20		28		62		N	16		21		39		76	
t	1.0		–		1.4		1.5		t	–		4.0		1.1		2.3	
p	NR		NR		<.05		<.05		p	NR		<.0003		NR		<.01	

Other evidence also indicates that the parents of repeated delinquents have lower job expectations for their sons. Parents were asked, "How much schooling do you think your son will really need for what he's likely to do when he's an adult?" Responses are summarized in Table 35. The parents of repeated delinquents judged their sons would need less education than did the parents of non-delinquents.

The picture of parental aspirations and expectations for their sons seems to be this: more parents in this study want their boy to enter the professions or other high prestige occupations than any other occupation. Most parents believe that if their son fails to achieve their aspirations for him it is the boy's failure, not to be blamed on forces external to him. The mothers of repeated delinquents, by more often professing belief in The American Dream, may be more ready than mothers of non-delinquents to find fault with their sons if the boys fall short of the targets set for them. When expectations are considered, however, the parents of repeated delinquents do not anticipate that their sons will achieve parental goals. It is probably a significant part of the situation of many repeated delinquent boys that their parents seem both to expect them to fall short and to stand ready to blame them for it. The evidence suggests that the positions taken by their parents are fertile grounds for the development of status problems among boys.

Table 36

Most boys believe in The American Dream of equal opportunity, delinquents and non-delinquents alike.

Question 31: Do you feel that every boy in this country has as good a chance as every other boy? Why do you say that?

School and the American Dream

Only the sons of white collar fathers were more skeptical about The Dream than their parents were, and there is a tendency for proportionally fewer of them to believe in The Dream than do sons of unskilled workers (see Table 36). It seems reasonable to conclude that white collar sons who disclaim belief feel they have advantages over their lower status peers, and data presented later suggest this is so. With white collar sons believing they have at least equal opportunities if not better, and most skilled and unskilled workers' sons believing in The American Dream, the following inference may be made: most boys seemed ready to blame themselves for failing to reach high status occupational levels.

These data on boys' beliefs in The American Dream prompt two observations. First, the assumption that boys generally compare themselves against "all comers" seems to be supported here, with the qualification that white collar boys may regard themselves in an advantageous position. Second, most boys do not seem to regard the status system as an important factor in their ultimate achievement of status. So while conditions are ripe for boys to develop status problems, it is not likely that these problems are perceived to flow from the status system directly. Often boys stated

Table 37

Both repeated delinquents and non-delinquents think of schooling mainly as a path to future opportunities, leading to better jobs or future.

Question 21c: Why don't you want to quit school when you're 16?

	R Likes School, Is Interested in Subjects	Needs Diploma to Get Good Job	Needs Diploma to Get to College	Keeps You Busy	Other	R Wants to Quit School	?	N
White collar								
Repeated delinquents	10%	45%	5%	--%	20%	5%	15%	20
Non-delinquents	5	45	20	--	20	5	5	20
Skilled								
Repeated delinquents	4	44	7	--	11	26	7	27
Non-delinquents	--	37	30	11	15	4	4	27
Unskilled								
Repeated delinquents	4	43	22	2	11	13	4	46
Non-delinquents	4	57	20	--	11	2	7	46
Total								
Repeated delinquents	5	44	14	1	13	15	8	93
Non-delinquents	3	48	23	3	14	3	5	93

explicitly that the fault was with boys themselves, and one particular shortcoming was often mentioned: "Some kids are smarter than
others in school. Some people get good grades and others bad
grades."

It seemed clear in the data that almost all the boys regarded
school as the gateway to bright occupational futures. Over half the
boys in the sample, the boys in the second and third columns of
Table 37, said that they didn't want to quit school because they
needed high school diplomas to get good jobs or to get into college.
When asked to select from among fixed alternatives the most important reason for going through high school, three-fourths of the boys
mentioned "to get a good job" or "to get into college" (see Table
38), while other reasons were chosen much less often. Repeated delinquents and non-delinquents shared this image of the function of
school in status achievement.

The importance of education to a future career appeared over
and over again throughout boys' interviews. One boy, denying the

Table 38

When asked to select the most important reason for completing
high school from a set of reasons, most repeated delinquents and
non-delinquents cite improvement in chances to get good jobs or
to go to college.

Question 17 (questionnaire): Which of these reasons for going
through high school do you think is most important?

	To Meet People; Make Friends	To Get a Good Job	To Get into College	To Keep Busy; Out of Trouble	To Learn How to Behave Right	To Have Fun	?	N
White collar								
Repeated delin-quents	--%	58%	37%	5%	--%	--%	--%	19
Non-delinquents	5	25	65	--	--	--	5	20
Skilled								
Repeated delin-quents	--	50	33	--	--	8	8	26
Non-delinquents	11	44	37	--	--	4	4	27
Unskilled								
Repeated delin-quents	7	52	22	7	2	4	7	46
Non-delinquents	2	47	37	2	2	--	9	43
Total								
Repeated delin-quents	3	53	29	4	1	4	6	91
Non-delinquents	7	47	30	9	--	2	5	90

reality of The American Dream, said, "Some guys get to go to college and some don't. The guys who go have their pick of jobs." Another boy, affirming The Dream, said, "The guy going through school has a better chance of getting a job than the guy who quits school." The reader may remember that non-delinquent Phil offered "good marks" as his first thought about what would help him gain the job he wanted. On the same subject, another boy said, "If I want a good job, I need to finish school."

A study of adolescents in Nashville, Tennessee, has also led sociologist A. J. Reiss (1959) to conclude that youngsters link success at school to life chances. He further found that lower-class youngsters regarded school as more important than did their middle-class peers, presumably because school achievement is more crucial to the success of lower-class children.

Many Flint parents struck the same theme. One mother, asked about her hopes for son's future, threw up her hands, saying, "I haven't had too much hope. He is not a good student. I am at my wit's end to guide him into a job. I want him to have a wife and family and be able to support them. He has to have some training with that in mind." The father of a repeated delinquent said if he could change anything at all about his son, "I'd like to make him more interested in school. He's going to need an education to get the kind of job he can do without hard physical labor."

School, Aspirations, Expectations, and Delinquency

With these perceptions of the dependency of future occupational status on school achievement, it is not surprising that boys' occupational aspirations varied with their school achievement records, as did their parents' aspirations for them. Table A-8 shows that among repeated delinquents and non-delinquents at all three social status levels, the higher a boy's average grade in junior high school, the higher his own present job aspirations and his parents' aspirations for him, although some of the correlations are admittedly very low. These data linking school success to their stated aspirations lend further strength to the inference that status problems are felt by most boys as personal failures, not as consequences of the social status system.

In order to link school achievement to delinquency, data were gathered on the grade averages of the boys in the core sample. An effort was made to obtain averages earned in years prior to a boy's first police contact so that factors associated with arrest and labeling as a "delinquent" would be ruled out. Fifth and seventh grade averages rather than the most recent averages were used for this reason. As Table 39 shows, repeated delinquents earn lower averages at both grade levels and at all social status levels; differences are reliable except in the one case of fifth grade averages for white collar sons. These differences in school grades between delinquents and non-delinquents show up despite the fact that matched boys are no more than ten points apart on I.Q. scores.

It is not surprising to find, then, that the aspirations of delinquent and non-delinquent boys differ. Boys were asked, "What job would you like to have when you take a job?" Their occupational choices were categorized according to the prestige system devised by W. L. Warner and his associates (op. cit.). At all three social status levels and most strongly among the sons of unskilled workers, repeated delinquents aspired to less prestigeful jobs. Table A-10 presents the boys' choices in the simpler form of U.S. Census occupational categories, but the differences between repeated delinquents and non-delinquents are apparent in this form, too. More non-delinquents reported professional aspirations, while the most usual

Table 39

Repeated delinquents are likely to have earned lower grades in the fifth and seventh grades than their non-delinquent matches.

	White Collar		Skilled		Unskilled		Total	
	Repeaters	Non-del.	Repeaters	Non-del.	Repeaters	Non-del.	Repeaters	Non-del.
Fifth Grade								
Average grade	2.5	2.6	2.2	2.6	2.2	2.5	2.3	2.5
N	15		19		26		60	
t	0.4		2.8		1.5		2.7	
p	NR		<.005		<.05		<.003	
Seventh Grade								
Average grade	2.0	2.3	1.5	2.2	1.4	2.0	1.5	2.1
N	13		22		39		74	
t	1.6		5.6		1.5		5.1	
p	<.05		<.0003		<.05		<.0003	

aspirations for repeated delinquents were to be craftsmen, foremen, or the like and, among repeated delinquent sons of unskilled workers, to be machine operators and such. It may be that boys adjust their aspirations to correspond to their level of achievement in school, and repeated delinquents, who perform less well in school, consequently have lower aspirations.

The correlations in Table A-8 showed that the higher a boy's grades in school, the higher his occupational aspirations tended to be. The correlations in Table A-9 demonstrate that the higher a boy's school grades, the better he views his chances of getting the

Table 40

There is little difference between repeated delinquents and non-delinquents in perceived chances of getting the jobs they want.

Question 28: What do you think your chances are of getting that job (you want) ?

Non-Delinquents (N=93)   Repeated Delinquents (N=93)

Very good (1)   27% / 20%

Fair (2)   30% / 45%

Even (3)   29% / 22%

Poor (4)   4% / 4%

Very bad (5)   0% / 0%

?   10% / 9%

	White Collar		Skilled		Unskilled		Total	
	Repeaters	Non-del.	Repeaters	Non-del.	Repeaters	Non-del.	Repeaters	Non-del.
Mean	1.6	1.9	2.3	2.1	2.2	2.1	2.09	2.05
N	30		42		82		154	
t	1.0		0.9		0.4		0.3	
p	NR		NR		NR		NR	

job he wants. The only reversal of this trend is among white collar repeated delinquents, and there the reversal is not strong enough
to make the correlation over all delinquents unreliable. Nevertheless, despite their lower grades, repeated delinquents do not differ
reliably from non-delinquents in their estimates of their chances of
getting the jobs they want, as Table 40 shows. How is it that their
lower school grades do not make the delinquent boys more pessi-
mistic about their life chances? It is here, perhaps, that lowering
job aspirations is revealed as a defense against feelings of personal
failure.

In those cases where there is a manifest discrepancy between
job aspirations and expectancies, coupled with a belief in The American Dream of equal opportunity for those with the will and skill,
then boys must feel inadequate. If poor school grades fix job expectancies at a relatively low level, then the only way to eradicate
this uncomfortable discrepancy is to lower aspirations. Many of
the repeated delinquents studied here may be doing just that, and
consequently the discrepancies between their job aspirations and expectancies are no larger than those of non-delinquents, contrary to
the original prediction.

Indeed, there is evidence in the data that lowering aspirations
tends to make delinquent boys more confident of their chances to
get the jobs they want. When boys were asked, within the context
of their belief in The American Dream, whether they themselves
had better, worse, or equal chances, delinquent boys felt their chances
were better than did non-delinquent boys (see Table 41). It should
be noted that this finding comes from white collar and skilled categories; there is no difference in the unskilled category. It seems
that lowering aspirations may overcompensate for feelings of impending failure among boys who are to be launched into the world
of occupations from a higher status level. Added evidence for this
is the fact, revealed in the reversed correlation in Table A-9, that
white collar repeated delinquents ignore, perhaps even defy their
school grades in estimating their chances at jobs they want.

These data help unravel the effects of status problems on delinquency. Data on their belief in The American Dream have been
interpreted to mean that boys are ready to perceive possible failure at status mobility as personal failure rather than as a consequence of the status system itself. Furthermore, personal failure
is generally linked to poor performance in school. It seems, then,
that the source and nature of the status problem may be identical
for higher status and lower status boys, so that status problems,
if they have any effect on delinquency at all, could lead to delinquency among higher status as well as lower status boys.

Table 41

White collar and skilled repeated delinquents are more confident
of their chances to get a good job than are matched non-delinquents, while no differences are apparent among the unskilled
workers' sons.

Question 31a: How about you ? Do you have a better, worse, or equal
chance ?

	White Collar		Skilled		Unskilled		Total	
	Repeat-ers	Non-del.	Repeat-ers	Non-del.	Repeat-ers	Non-del.	Repeat-ers	Non-del.
Mean	1.6	1.9	1.9	2.2	1.9	1.9	1.8	1.9
N	15		11		21		47	
t	1.7		1.9		--		1.7	
p	<.05		<.03		NR		<.03	

The pattern of the data point to the possibility that status
problems are not manifested in discrepancies between occupational
aspirations and expectations, but rather in psychologically comfort-
ing downgradings of aspirations. The interpretation of repeated delinquents' lower aspirations as defensive is an inference which fits
the data to the general theory of status problems as provocative to
delinquency. Still, it is possible that lower aspirations do not represent defenses but are in fact indicative either of realistic appraisals

or of underlying differences in values between delinquents and non-delinquents.

If lower aspirations represent the effect of greater realism on the part of repeated delinquents, still the discrepancy between what these boys would ideally like to do and the jobs they will probably get remains as a provocation to delinquency. Whether lower aspirations are defensive or realistic is not crucial to the issue of whether a discrepancy between the ideal and the probable exists. Frankly, however, the interpretations of defensiveness is favored here for several reasons. First, data on The American Dream do not distinguish delinquents as more realistic than non-delinquents; about as many of each group believe in The Dream. Second, when boys were asked, "How sure are you about wanting that job?" delinquents were as sure as their matched non-delinquents. Third, it seems reasonable to suppose that a provocation to delinquency must be fairly powerful to overcome the resistance against it, and according to psychoanalytic theory at least, defensive forces are apt to be more powerful than realistic ones.

The interpretation of lower aspirations as a reflection of differences in real preferences about jobs does threaten a theory based on discrepancies between the ideal and the possible; for if repeated delinquents actually prefer the less prestigeful jobs, then no discrepancy exists at any level. This interpretation is the kind suggested by Walter B. Miller, whose theory about delinquency was outlined in Chapter II. Looked at in this way, lower aspirations might suggest a source of weakened controls rather than a source of provocations insofar as they demonstrate that values held by most of the larger society are not shared by delinquents.

However, other data suggest that repeated delinquents do not differ from non-delinquents in their judgments of the status of various occupations. The boys in this study were asked to rate jobs on a four-point scale from "excellent" to "poor." Table A-11 shows that repeated delinquents rate occupations in very much the same order as do non-delinquents and a representative U.S. population.

There is reason to believe that boys' perceptions of life chances are sources of weakened social controls as well as of provocations. It has been proposed that the possibility of a police record spoiling a boy's chances at a good job might keep him from becoming delinquent. Data presented in Table 42 indicate that about half the boys interviewed did feel that a police record hurt a boy's life chances, and another fourth felt this was so under some conditions. It has been suggested that repeated delinquents less often believe

Table 42

Many boys believe that a police record would affect their life-chances.

Question 43: If a boy had been in trouble with the police, do you think this would make any difference to what he might want or be able to do in the future?

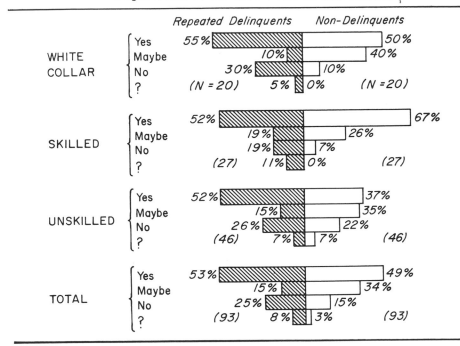

they have good chances to spoil; they tend to think they have already spoiled their own chances. So the threat of a police record probably does not serve as a controlling function for repeated delinquents as it does for non-delinquents, and it may account in part for the former having acquired police records.

Still another way in which differential life chances may create differential social controls involves the school as a controlling institution. Here the element of attraction enters again, on the assumption that boys who perform less well in school are less attracted to it and consequently, less controlled by it. The assumed relationship of school performance and attraction to school appears to be well founded, according to the data in Table 43. The first column contains the Pearson correlation coefficients between boys' attitudes toward school and their seventh grade averages, while the second column demonstrates that the relationships indicated by the correlations are reliable. The trend is the same at all three social strata, although the data are not shown separately for each stratum. Perhaps even more significant in Table 43 is the correlation of .40 between repeated delinquents' attitudes toward school and their perceived life chances: the less likely it seemed they would get the jobs they wanted, the less they liked school. The same relationship holds, but less strongly, for non-delinquents. School seems in part to be attractive to boys to the extent that it improves their life chances.

Table 43

Boys' attitudes toward school are more positive when their grades are higher and when they think they have better chances to get jobs they want.

| | Attitudes toward School, and | | | |
| | Seventh Grade Averages | | Perceived Job Chances | |
	r	p-level (2t)	r	p-level (2t)
Repeated delinquents	.25	<.01	.40	<.005
Non-delinquents	.21	<.05	.26	<.01

Another indication that school may be less attractive to repeated delinquents and therefore have less potential control over them is in the data of Table 44. Repeated delinquents did not believe their teachers were as interested in their futures as did non-delinquents. Again, although a complete breakdown of the data is not given here, the pattern is the same among boys at each status level.

It seems legitimate to conclude that status problems are more characteristic of repeated delinquents than non-delinquents and that they may indeed provoke boys to delinquency. It also seems likely that poor school performance functions both to set the conditions for status problems and to reduce the potential of school as a controlling institution. Furthermore, the process seems to be similar for higher and lower status boys. It is necessary now to consider how these findings may help to explain the greater incidence of delinquency among lower status boys, the central problem for this research.

Table 44

Repeated delinquents less often than matched non-delinquents feel
that their teachers take a great deal of interest in their futures.

Question 18 (questionnaire): How much interest do you feel your
teachers have taken in your future?

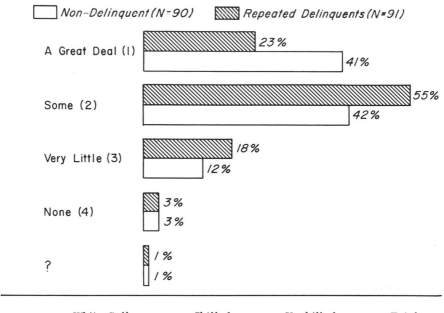

	White Collar		Skilled		Unskilled		Total	
	Repeaters	Non-del.	Repeaters	Non-del.	Repeaters	Non-del.	Repeaters	Non-del.
Mean	2.0	1.9	2.2	1.8	1.9	1.8	2.0	1.8
N	19		25		44		88	
t	0.8		2.2		0.6		1.9	
p	NR		<.01		NR		<.03	

Social Status and School Performance

It was originally proposed that lower status boys might be provoked to delinquency by the relatively poor life chances afforded to
those in their status positions, and that higher status boys might be
less controlled because their futures did not depend so much on their

present behavior. The data gathered in this study suggest that most boys do not perceive their life chances as a function of the social system itself but as a function of their personal characteristics. Therefore, in order to link social status with provocation to delinquency, it seems necessary to posit that personal failure is more likely to occur among lower status boys; specifically, that more lower status boys perform poorly in school than higher status boys. This link between social status and delinquency is, in fact, fairly firm, since the data indicate that lower status boys more often do fail at their schoolwork. Seventh grade averages, presented in Table 39, diminish among both repeated delinquents and non-delinquents from the highest average among white collar men's boys to the lowest among unskilled workers' sons. It has been pointed out, however, that the sample of boys taken for this research is not representative of social strata, so supportive evidence from elsewhere is desirable. P. Sexton's data on Detroit schools and school children (Sexton, *op. cit.*) indicate that 41 per cent of the children in lower status schools have failures on their records, while only 29 per cent of those in higher status schools have ever failed. A. Hollingshead (1949) reported that in a mid-western community he called Elmtown, youngsters of lower social status did less well in school. D. C. Shaw (1943) got the same results in his study of school performance among children in different social strata.

Furthermore, lower status youngsters seem to respond generally to their poorer school performance as the repeated delinquents studied here apparently do. W. F. Grunes (1956), reporting a study of students in eight high schools around the United States, asserted that those in lower socio-economic strata seem actually to avoid a choice of occupations. "When reality intrudes, however, they do not aim as high as do students in upper classes. Nevertheless, they rate themselves as less confident than others about attaining even their inferior goals." Grunes also noted the working of this process among higher status students.

> Students, even of high social status, who say their teachers would rate their ability as only fair or poor, are similar to the lower status group. . . . Thus feeling oneself to be an academic failure seems to have effects on vocational thinking which are similar to those in a low social class.

Since lower status boys are more likely to fail at school, it may be inferred that they are more likely to experience status problems which are provocative to delinquent behavior. The data in Table 43 suggest that school failure weakens attractions to school, so lower status boys are less likely to be controlled effectively by school personnel. It may also be true that the negative attitudes of some teachers toward teaching lower status youngsters, suggested by data on resignations in Chapter V, are communicated to these boys and contributes to weakened attractions and weakened social controls. J. K. Myers and B. H. Roberts (1959) found that lower status mental patients more often than higher status patients said they had not liked their childhood teachers and thought their teachers had not liked them. One patient said, "If you was poor they treated you different. Maybe they were supposed to treat all the kids the same, but they didn't. I guess I hated all teachers." Putting this clue together with the data on school achievement and occupational aspirations suggests that the whole process involving provocations and controls related to status problems and school is more likely to occur among lower status boys and generate a higher delinquency rate among them.

Aspirations and Achievement: The Causal Process

Throughout the discussion of data in this chapter, it has been assumed that poor achievement in school prompts boys to lower their occupational aspirations. It may actually be the case however, that low aspirations cause poor school performance. At the moment, this is an open question; no data presented here or anywhere else as far as it could be ascertained, help to settle this issue. The crucial point to be made here is that repeated delinquents are more vulnerable to feelings of personal failure, whether their school achievement leads to low aspirations or not.

Summary

The analysis reported in this chapter was begun for the purpose of testing the theory, largely derived from A. K. Cohen's work, that lower status boys more often became delinquent because the American social system disadvantaged them in their striving for higher status and provoked them to delinquent behavior as a reaction against relatively inaccessible status symbols. Further, middle class boys were hypothesized to become delinquent because their relatively assured futures implied weakened social controls.

As the data were ordered, however, the theory underwent significant modifications. It appeared that conditions were ripe for status problems among boys: most parents and boys were concerned about the occupational future, and many parents had high occupational aspirations for their sons. General belief in The American

Dream by parents and boys made it doubtful that the social system was perceived as the source of status problems. Rather, parents seemed ready to hold boys personally responsible for impending failure to rise socially. Further, the intimate connection perceived to link school performance to occupational chances suggested that poor academic records foretold status mobility failure. It was inferred that boys reacted to their poor performances in school and the consequent likelihood of mobility failure by lowering their occupational aspirations. Nevertheless, their attitudes toward different occupations still reflected acceptance of widely held prestige criteria concerning wealth and power. While certain boys lowered their aspirations, they were apparently aspiring to occupations they themselves regarded as of low status. While it was originally assumed that status problems would manifest themselves in discrepancies between occupational aspirations and expectations, the data suggested that such discrepancies were too threatening to boys to be maintained and disappeared in what is held here to be defensive aspirational downgradings. Status problems therefore seemed to be signaled by lower aspiration levels.

Repeated delinquents from white collar, skilled, and unskilled workers' families more often exhibited status problems than nondelinquents. That is, most of them had performed less well in school than their matched controls and had presumably lowered their aspirations to relieve felt status problems. But it appeared that status problems nevertheless remained potent enough to provoke delinquent behaviors. At the same time, relative failure in school seemed not only indirectly to provoke them to delinquency, it also may have weakened their attraction to school and consequently may have weakened the control school might exercise over them. Moreover, the lack of an occupational future which they deemed worthwhile could have been a factor weakening community controls over the boys who became repeated delinquents.

The most important implication of this chapter is that provocations and weakened social controls relevant to delinquency seem to be generated by the same process for both lower and higher status boys. Personal failure at school appears to be a part of the lives of repeated delinquents much more often than of non-delinquents and seems to have a significant effect on their perceptions of their life chances, whatever their social status. The impact of personal failure is probably felt by more lower status boys and may explain the greater incidence of delinquency among them; at the same time, personal failure and consequent status problems may provoke much of the delinquency committed by higher status boys.

Chapter VIII

DIRECTION OF CAUSAL PROCESSES

Studies which compare known delinquents with non-delinquents have at least one grave weakness: it is possible that any differences such studies discover are consequences of delinquency, not forerunners. To be apprehended by police for breaking the law and to be identified and labeled as a juvenile delinquent is a significant experience in a boy's life. It may be argued that such an experience would alter a boy's attitudes toward himself and environment, his family life patterns, and so on. The differences found by a study comparing known delinquents to non-delinquents are often interpreted, however, as signals of or precursors to delinquency which are then strongly suggested to be causes. Yet, these differences may be created by the event of police apprehension and may not have existed previous to the delinquent act at all.

It is possible, for example, that the father-son relationship, rather than being a crucial factor in the breakdown of social control over a boy, is especially disrupted by the boy's delinquent behavior and the shame and guilt fathers feel when the police call to have him fetch his son from jail. Thereupon may follow repressive disciplinary measures, distance between father and son, and loss of control which, at the boy's first adoption of a delinquent pattern, may have been minor or perhaps nonexistent elements in their relationship.

Perhaps the attitudes a boy expresses toward his family, his neighborhood, his school, and his community are results, not causes of his delinquency. It may be that his delinquent behavior sprang from quite other sources, but once having established a behavior pattern with repeated offenses and having been stamped as a "juvenile delinquent," the boy began to act the role as he had seen it portrayed on television and in the movies. Perhaps he was still behaving as he thought a delinquent ought to behave when the smart college boy quizzed him for the Flint Youth Study.

The question this chapter discusses is: To what extent are the findings of this study a consequence of boys and parents adopting

174

behaviors and distorting memories *after* the boys' repeated apprehensions for serious offenses?   In an attempt to answer this question, the sample of non-delinquents and of sometime delinquents, the one-time offenders, was followed up from a year to a year and a half after their interviews were taken.   The idea was to isolate those boys who later qualified as repeated delinquents and to compare their prior interview responses with those of boys who did not become delinquent. This strategy might be considered a short-term longitudinal design. Perhaps the boys who became repeated delinquents after they were interviewed had earlier behaved in some ways like the already known repeaters had behaved; then at least the priority of certain behaviors would be established.   While priority is no guarantee of causality, it would confirm that repeated police apprehension did not produce the findings reported.

The Nature of the Sometime Delinquent Category

It will be helpful here to recall the nature of the sometime delinquent sample.   It consists of 43 boys who were contacted by the police for only one serious offense committed within the three years previous to the study; these boys were matched with pairs of repeated delinquent and non-delinquent boys.   It has been assumed that the sometime delinquent sample includes both repeated delinquent boys who had not yet been caught twice and essentially non-delinquent boys who seriously misbehaved once but would not do so again.   Putting it another way, the sometime delinquents presumably include both boys for whom delinquency was a patterned way of life and boys whose delinquent behaviors were spontaneous acts depending heavily on particular situations.

Thirteen New Repeated Delinquents

A review of the police contact files from 12 to 17 months after the boys were interviewed turned up five non-delinquents who had in that period committed at least two serious offenses and eight sometime delinquents who had committed at least one more.   The most serious behavior one of these boys had shown previously, according to his father, had been an incident of shop-lifting a knife about six years earlier; six months after he and his family had been interviewed, the youngster broke into a store and stole some merchandize, and six months after that he assaulted an adult on a Flint side street in an attempt at robbery.   Another non-delinquent had one record of running his motor scooter through a stop sign; 14 months after he had been interviewed, this youngster stole three cars in as many months.   These were the nature of the delinquencies which qualified the 13 boys for the repeated delinquent category.   Table 45 summarizes the follow-up cases.

Table 45

A review of the police files from 12 to 19 months after boys had been interviewed revealed that delinquents were six times more likely than non-delinquents to have committed another serious offense.

	Non-Delinquents	Sometime Delinquents	Repeated Delinquents
No further police record	86	35	63[a]
Additional police record of a serious nature	5[b]	8	30
Total	91[c]	43	93

a. This figure includes two drunks and a parole violator whose offense was not otherwise a serious delinquency.

b. Two non-delinquents committed one serious offense; three committed two or more.

c. Two boys were, in the follow-up, revealed to have been misclassified as non-delinquents, one having had one offense and the other two offenses in the police files.

The Delinquent-like Index

It was necessary to select behavior items on which to compare the new group of repeated delinquents with the remaining non-delinquents and sometime delinquents.   Two criteria were used to select items: First, they were to include only boys' behaviors and attitudes, rather than variables like social status, broken homes, attitudes of parents, etc., so as to be consistent with the orientation that the causes of delinquency are to be found in the provocations and social controls created in boys themselves by these other factors.   Second, they were to include only those factors which had distinguished repeated delinquents from non-delinquents, since this follow-up design was intended to test alternative explanations for these findings.

Eleven items were selected according to these criteria, two of them indicators of what has been taken here to be a major provocation to delinquency, and the rest, indicators of the strength of social control.   The two provocation items were (1) occupational aspiration and (2) seventh grade average.   The nine social control items were (3) agreement with father about how he ought to behave, (4) agreement with mother about how he ought to behave, (5) who he takes personal problems to, (6) perception of his model's approval of delinquent acts, (7) attitude toward Flint, (8) attitude toward neighborhood, (9) attitude toward school, (10) perceptions of his teachers' interest in his future, and (11) acceptance of father as an adult model.

Each item was dichotomized into a delinquent and non-delinquent response. For example, repeated delinquents were found more often to disagree with the statement, "When I become an adult, I'd like to be the kind of person my father is," so disagreement was considered the delinquent-like response to this item. Each boy was then assigned one point for each delinquent-like response he gave, so that the more points he scored, the more he could be considered delinquent-like at his initial interview. However, since some boys did not respond to some items, the percentage of points each boy earned over the total possible for him was the score ultimately used. This means that a completely delinquent-like boy scored 100, while a completely non-delinquent boy scored 0.

Since the scoring system was based on found differences in responses of repeated delinquents compared to non-delinquents, of course boys in these two categories scored very differently. Table 46 demonstrates that the percentage of non-delinquents surpasses that of repeated delinquents only in the first column, containing the lowest range of scores.

Table 46

An index composed of items which distinguished the attitudes and behaviors of repeated delinquents from those of non-delinquents proves also to place sometime delinquents between these two categories and to be related to social status.

DELINQUENCY CATEGORIES:	RANGE OF POINTS ON INDEX[a]					N
	0-20	21-40	41-60	61-80	81-100	
	(low)				(high)	
Repeated Delinquents	14%	34%	30%	18%	3%	93
Sometime Delinquents	23%	35%	30%	12%	0%	43
Non-Delinquents	46%	34%	14%	5%	0%	93
SOCIAL STATUS CATEGORIES:[b]						N
White Collar	48%	20%	25%	7%	0%	40
Skilled Workers	31%	33%	20%	12%	4%	54
Unskilled Workers	22%	41%	22%	14%	1%	92

a. See text for items included in index.
b. Includes only repeated and non-delinquents.

The scoring system merits some degree of confidence, however, by the way it places the sometime delinquents and by its relationship to social status. Table 47 demonstrates that sometime delinquents fall between repeated delinquents and non-delinquents on the delinquent-like score; this is just where they should fall if in fact the sometime delinquent group comprised a mixture of undetected and potential repeaters as well as essentially non-delinquent boys. It should be pointed out, however, that the average delinquent-like score of the sometime delinquents falls closer to the average score of their repeated delinquent matches than to the average score of their non-delinquent matches. The difference in the former case just misses the reliability level set for this study, while the latter difference is clearly reliable.

Table 47

Non-delinquents and sometime delinquents who commit delinquencies subsequent to being interviewed tend to have had higher scores on a delinquent-like index than matched boys who commit no more delinquencies.

Scores on Predictive Index	Boys Who Commit Delinquencies after Being Interviewed	Median Scores of Matched Boys Who Do Not Commit Delinquencies after Being Interviewed	N upon Which Median is Based	Difference Scores
(1)[a]	20	33	17	−13
(2)[a]	40	30	13	10
(3)[a]	30	18	4	12
(4)[a]	18	25.5	6	− 7.5
(5)	80	18	10	62
(6)	27	29.5	4	− 2.5
(7)	10	9	2	1
(8)	36	43.5	2	− 7.5
(9)	70	40	3	30
(10)	55	42.5	4	13.5
(11)	36	43.5	2	− 7.5
(12)	56	9	1	47
(13)	70	14.5	4	56.5

	Delinquents		Non-Delinquents
Mean	42.2		27.4
N		26	
t		2.1	
p		<.03	

a. Originally non-delinquents; the rest were sometime delinquents.

Moreover, boys in the white collar category tend to score lower than boys in the skilled category, who in turn score lower than boys in the unskilled category (only repeated delinquents and non-delinquents are included in the social class breakdown to insure an equal number of each at each social status level); the relationship of the delinquent-like score to social status is consistent with the hypothesis that the factors which are closely related to delinquency more frequently appear among lower status boys.   It seemed justifiable to continue this approach to causality with some confidence in the delinquent-like index.

Data from the Delinquent-like Index

The fact that only 13 boys made up the sample of new repeated delinquents posed a problem of a comparison group for the analysis. If 13 boys were picked at random to match with these 13 new delinquents, it would be quite possible to select among those 13 controls some boys whose delinquent-like scores were abnormally low or abnormally high.   With as few boys as 13, one or two extreme scores could significantly push the results in one direction or another.   Some step had to be taken to stabilize the sample of boys with whom the new repeated delinquents were matched.   So all the possible matches for each boy were sorted out: against each new repeated delinquent was arrayed all the boys in the sample of approximately the same age, the same I.Q., at the same school level, whose fathers had the same status job, and who had had the same number of police contacts—none or one—at the time of interviewing.   The number of matches for each boy ranged from 1 to 17 boys.   The median delinquent-like score of the matches, more representative of all the boys who had not become repeated delinquents than the score of any of them, was compared to the score of the new repeated delinquent. Table 47 presents the results of the analysis.

In 8 of the 13 pairs, the new repeated delinquent had a higher delinquent-like score than the median score of his controls.   This result in itself is not especially impressive, but it is also clear that the differences in these pairs are generally larger than the differences in the other five pairs.   The t-test of differences between means indicates that these differences among the scores of the 13 pairs could have occurred by chance in the direction found only 3 times out of 100.

Summary

The data presented here suggest that the differences found between repeated delinquents and non-delinquents were not due to changes in attitudes and behaviors subsequent to delinquency. The responses of boys who had not yet been apprehended twice, some not even once, on the whole demonstrated delinquent-like attitudes and behavior. Non-delinquents and even sometime delinquents who did not repeat their delinquent behaviors had generally responded differently from those who became repeated delinquents. It seems reasonable to conclude that the factors present in the psychological structure of repeated delinquents were present before they became officially delinquent. It has been pointed out that this conclusion does not lead easily to assertions of causality; it is, however, a step in that direction.

The data presented in this brief chapter must be recognized as especially flimsy. Even steps to stabilize a closely matched comparison group do not overcome completely the small number of boys who were relevant to the problem. If and when some more elaborate longitudinal study becomes possible, it may be worthwhile to test the delinquent-like index on a wider sample of youngsters.

Chapter IX

FROM THE PRESENT STANDPOINT

This work began with two questions, an orientation, and some possible answers. The questions probed into the relationship between social status and juvenile delinquency. The orientation was social-psychological. Possible answers posited provocations to and controls over delinquency in processes which involved boys and their society, their community, and their families. In the course of the research, some of the possible answers gained precedence over others and some new possibilities became apparent. This concluding chapter is comprised of a brief statement of the standpoint to which this research has led and a consideration of next steps which might be taken from the present position. The prevention and treatment of delinquency is discussed in the context of action research.

The Present Standpoint

This work first has added still another set of data to those which support the contention that proportionately more lower status boys commit delinquent acts than do their higher status peers. The data offered here are more pertinent than most of those already found in the literature since they were taken from police contact files; thereby they avoid some of the social status biases which these present data themselves demonstrate to occur in delinquency statistics based on arrests, court cases, and institutionalizations. The effect of these data is to legitimize a search for processes which link lower social status to delinquency.

The theoretical position from which this search began proposed that forces relevant to delinquency might be classified as controlling or provoking forces. The controlling forces were hypothesized to consist most importantly of attractions to norm-supporting individuals and organizations. The greatest potential for control was assumed to be the family group and within it, the attractiveness of the father was expected to be most crucial. Attractiveness of the community was also investigated as a basis for control, especially with regard

181

to the attractiveness of its recreational and educational facilities. The provocative force peculiar to delinquency was hypothesized to be status deprivation; that is, boys' feelings that they would not achieve positions of wealth and power which are considered prestigeful in their society. Delinquency is an ideal solution for status deprivation problems because, according to Cohen's theory, delinquent behavior simultaneously repudiates the societal values by which boys are to regard themselves as failures and wins status for boys among peers who share these status problems.

Over-representation of lower status boys among delinquents, it was proposed, occurs because the conditions of lower status tend to weaken the attractions which are sources of controls and tend to strengthen the provocation of status deprivation. However, it was expected that the same conditions would appear, albeit with less frequency, among higher status boys, among whom they would also generate delinquency.

Some possible linking processes have been isolated. It should be pointed out immediately that these particular process-links were found because the research was aimed in their direction. Probably others were missed. So these processes are probably not all there are, and continued research will most likely uncover more.

One major link found between social status and delinquency among the boys studied here involves their performance in school. One interpretation of the result is that when boys do poorly at their schoolwork they are likely to become convinced that they are and will continue to be failures. Since they and their parents regard success at school as an important stepping stone in the path to higher status jobs and since they also regard this path open to anyone skilled enough and motivated enough to travel it, school failure generates a feeling of personal inadequacy. Their school careers themselves are instances of failure, but perhaps more important, their inability to do well in school presages failure in the adult world of occupations, which, following A. K. Cohen, has here been identified as a status problem.

Provocative status problems are more likely to occur among lower status boys. On the one hand, these boys are more likely to fail at school for lack of the cultural background conducive to success in that higher status institution; and on the other hand, school failure is a surer sign of dim occupational chances for boys lacking financial and other status-linked resources for getting ahead. However, perhaps the most important implication of this study is that delinquency among higher status boys seems to follow upon the same set of provocative circumstances; but delinquency occurs less often among higher status boys because fewer of them are subject to such status problems.

Just as lower status boys are more often provoked to delinquency by status problems, social controls against delinquency seem likely to be weaker among them. Their families, the primary agencies for social control, are probably generally less attractive to them, especially because their fathers seem to be less attractive to them. The same social criteria which generate status problems for boys provide them with standards of success against which to evaluate their families and especially their breadwinners. Where attraction is weak, the social control which is built upon it has weak potential. Again, the same dynamics seem to occur among higher status delinquent boys.

Some but not all provocative forces are also instances of weakened controls. School failure with consequent status problems has been tentatively identified as a primary provocation to delinquency; and weak family attractiveness, as a primary source of weak social control against delinquency. In addition, each factor may have an effect like the other. Boys who are convinced that they will not achieve status in their society may consequently feel that they have no worthwhile opportunities to lose by becoming identified as delinquents; boys who do poorly in school are probably less attracted to and therefore less amenable to the influence of school personnel. The intertwining of these factors, all around a central thread of status which is concomitantly personal and social, strengthens the conviction that they may in fact underlie delinquency; for it probably requires a multiplicity of forces, an overdetermination of motivations, to drive boys to repeated seriously deviant behaviors.

Another control factor seems to be the way boys are disciplined when they misbehave: boys who are punished physically or deprived of something, by their fathers, seem consequently to be less attracted to their fathers. They also may learn from their punishment that appropriate behavior when angry is to strike out against another. Again, these types of punishment, rather than the more guilt-inducing reasoning and rejecting practices, are more prevalent among parents in lower social strata and among parents of delinquent boys. They probably add impetus to aggression against external objects once such aggression is initiated by other provocations, and they seem to weaken social controls.

As this work began with a rejection of a single-cause approach to delinquency, so its progress has strengthened this rejection.

Lewin insisted that all choice behaviors are consequences of patterns of determinants, or fields of forces. Delinquency seems to be no exception. The answer to the question—Why do proportionately more lower status boys become delinquent than do higher status boys?—seems to be this: some of the related variables which are important in determining delinquent behavior more often occur in the lives of lower status boys, and so the probability that they will occur in some pattern which actually produces delinquency is greater among lower status boys. These delinqeuncy-producing patterns are not always the same; indeed, each is as unique as the boy whom it characterizes. But the data suggest that status problem provocations and weak familial controls may very often be part of these patterns. It also appears that the patterns which determine delinquency among higher status boys are no more different from the patterns among lower status boys than they are from one another.

A direct implication of this pattern approach is that it is merely a research technique to separate boys into exclusive categories of delinquents and non-delinquents. Psychologically, delinquency may be a relative matter. Forces for and against delinquency are probably at work in every youngster. Their strength, probably in combination with opportunities available, may determine whether a boy will commit a delinquent act, but the act may be only the overt symptom of a boy's psychological state. Some boys who are never delinquent may be very close to the critical point while others may be far from it; some who become delinquent may be just past the critical point and others may be far beyond it. The strengths and weaknesses of these forces which make up a psychological pattern relevant to delinquency may be only roughly reflected in the frequency and seriousness of a boy's delinquent behaviors.

It should be clear that the present standpoint is a tentative position. To begin with, all the findings reported have been offered in probability terms. No factor has differentiated all delinquents from all non-delinquents. While the probabilities of actual relationships have been statistically high, this is no guarantee that they will not prove in future research to have been chance occurrences. This is only one reason for tentativeness. Another is that it is difficult to estimate the importance of the phenomena studied here in the determination of delinquency. Perhaps the variables which seemed to make a difference were peculiar to the boys and their families who were interviewed. Perhaps, although statistical differences were reliably large, they were differences which make very little difference; that is, the variables isolated here may really be peripheral to and only symptomatic of the central causes of delinquency. Just as the present findings gained support from previous research, so they will be strengthened or weakened by work still to be done.

Next Steps

One way of testing the validity of the present standpoint is to see how well it accounts for other juvenile delinquency phenomena. For example, it is fairly well established that Negro youngsters are responsible for a greater proportion of delinquency than their proportion in the population (cf. Neumeyer, *op. cit.*, pp. 178-181). Factors such as status problems and familial control might help to explain this fact: for certainly Negro youngsters do less well than whites in school and more frequently have fathers whose low prestige jobs may lower their attractiveness; and certainly Negro boys may easily and justifiably become convinced that they will not achieve a high level of social status. But do Negro boys regard their impending status failure as personal failure or do they attribute it to social arrangements; that is, do Negro boys and their parents subscribe to The American Dream? And is the relative frequency of fatherless homes a source of weakened social controls?

What about girls? It seems clear from the literature that girls are not so often delinquent as boys (cf. *ibid.*, p. 28), and that lower status girls are more likely to commit delinquent acts than higher status girls, with status differences perhaps even more pronounced among girls than among boys (Thomas, 1937). Now occupational success is presumably not so salient for girls as for boys, and relationships with fathers should not, according to psychoanalytic theory at least, be so important for social control among girls as their relationships with mothers. These considerations imply that the processes which have been isolated here are specific to boys and do not pertain to girls. On the other hand, it is possible that, with appropriate transformations, status problems and weakened familial controls can be found to determine girls' delinquency too.

Life chances among girls in our culture may reasonably be assumed to depend largely upon whom they marry. If a girl marries a higher status boy, she shares that status with him; if she marries a boy who is socially mobile, she is mobile with him. But it may also be assumed that a lower status girl's chances of marrying someone of higher status is not so great as girls who are themselves higher status. On this account, perhaps lower status girls are beset with status problems parallel to those of lower status boys. This argument suggests, however, that unlike most boys, most girls might attribute their status problems to status position disadvantages rather than to personal failure. Or is there such a thing as The American Dream: Marriage Version? It becomes crucial to learn whom girls want to marry and whom they expect to marry, and whether social status is a factor in their choices. One item of data suggests that this line of thinking is worth following up: delinquency among girls is more likely to involve sexual misbehavior than does delinquency among boys (*ibid.*). Perhaps such misbehavior symbolically repudiates just those marriage-related criteria which derogate lower status girls, in a fashion identical to the acts against wealth and power more common among male delinquents.

Perhaps the processes which weaken social control among delinquent girls are also similar to the process which seems to operate among delinquent boys. For example, girls may emulate their mothers in part because of the success they have been able to achieve, that is, because of the status of the men they have married and the status symbols—house, clothes, and so forth—which are consequently theirs. What are the criteria by which girls choose adult models? Do mother-daughter relationships in fact play the important part in the delinquent prodrome of girls?

Another way in which the present standpoint can be tested pertains to the phenomena of exceptionally low delinquency rates among certain ethnic groups. The Japanese, Chinese (*ibid.*, p. 184) and Jews (Kvaraceus, 1945, p. 405) have maintained low delinquency rates despite their minority group status and despite periods in their history in America when they were for the most part in lower socio-economic strata. The present standpoint provides a few leads to explain their low rates. On the one hand, it appears that the cultures of all three of these groups includes a scholarly tradition. There are strong prescriptions that children, especially sons, become as well educated as possible, and families are enjoined to prepare and encourage their youngsters to perform well in school. It is possible that this culturally derived motivational force is sufficient to overcome barriers to school achievement inherent in foreignness and in lower status so that Japanese, Chinese, and Jewish boys have not demonstrated the incidence of school failure of other comparable groups of boys. If so, then what appears at this time to be a major source of provocation to delinquency would thereby be minimized.

Another possible lead is the culturally determined position of fathers in Japanese, Chinese, and Jewish families. Perhaps fathers, bolstered by tradition, could withstand the attacks upon their power positions made by the economic circumstances surrounding them as recent immigrants. If so, fathers might then have better served as objects of their sons' emulation and consequently as sources of social control. Do the fathers in these ethnic groups wield greater influence in their families than men in comparable groups? Do their sons tend to respect them more? Research may reveal different patterns among ethnic groups which, from the present standpoint, are directly relevant to delinquency rates among them.

Is Delinquency "Abnormal"?

It is not hard to see why delinquency is regarded as abnormal. Certainly it is not normal in the sense that it is usual. For example, only about one in every ten Flint boys is a repeated delinquent on the official records. So it seems reasonable to conclude that an abnormal event, delinquency, depends on abnormal circumstances. But this is just the conclusion which is unacceptable from the present standpoint.

None of the factors which have been found here to be important in a delinquency-producing pattern are particularly *unusual*. School failure, low aspirations, and low social status; low status of fathers' jobs, physical and deprivational types of punishment, and broken homes; relatively poor recreational and educational facilities —none of these is exceptionally rare. What is relatively rare is the simultaneous occurrence of many of these in the life of a single boy. The present standpoint is that it takes a pattern of delinquency-producing factors to generate delinquent behavior, and these patterns fortunately do not occur very often.

Nor are any of these factors abnormal in the sense that they are wholly undesirable and spring from undesirable conditions. Each of these factors is a part of accepted social processes. For example, the relationship between school achievement and life chances is part of the technological stage of development which the civilized world has attained. This developmental stage requires and therefore rewards certain occupational skills. In this context, it is neither practicable nor desirable to destroy the school-job relationship. Still, its existence creates among school failures forces which appear to help generate delinquency. Nor is it likely that our schools can arrange to have no failures; for as long as different levels of school achievement serve as an index of occupational potential and as long as different school achievement and occupational levels are differentially rewarded, school failures are the inherent outcome of what is essentially the most democratic educational system we have as yet been able to construct.

Another example of how delinquency may be an outcome of accepted social process is in the way father-son relationships are affected by social criteria. It has been suggested that a father's occupational status as a symbol of success directly affects his attractiveness to his son.   Now the criteria by which boys measure their fathers' success are not unusual nor are they different from delinquent to non-delinquent boys; they are part of the social system in which they live.   Still, status factors not infrequently create father-son relationships too weak to withstand provocations to delinquency.

One point to be made here is this: large-scale prevention of delinquency probably depends on large-scale changes in the social system.   Delinquency is not abnormal in that system, but a certain level of delinquency is inherent in it.   Since large-scale changes in the social system are not likely to occur, certainly not in order to reduce delinquency, it does not seem that much hope can be invested in delinquency prevention.

Treatment is another matter.   The first step may be to think of treatment, not as correcting abnormalities, but in locating and correcting instances where normal processes have compounded to produce delinquency.   Formulated in this way, treatment programs become corrective mechanisms in the social system aimed to reclaim some of that system's natural but undesirable products.   Treatment would then properly begin in watchfulness; this necessitates sharpening the detection of delinquency where it occurs, and the detection of existing conditions which most likely are about to generate delinquency.   The next step would be to apply techniques specific to the major causes of the target delinquency; this necessitates perfecting techniques for treating specific patterns of delinquency causation on the social organizational and on the individual levels.

Hopefully this work has made a few steps, just a few and short ones at that, toward a more complete understanding of delinquency specifically and of human behavior generally.   It is difficult at this time to measure the distance traveled except to recognize that it has been quite short.   And there is always the possibility that the steps taken have been false ones after all.   Only continued research can provide an accurate perspective on the present work.   Meanwhile, this, as any other of a scientific nature, must be regarded as a tentative and interim report.

APPENDIX I

THE MATCHED SAMPLE

Code[1]	Birthdate	I.Q.	Father's Occupation
0020	8-13-41	104	Stock handler
0021	5-6-42	101	Set-up man
0022	7-14-41	105	Operative
0030	12-21-42	87	Sewer cleaner
0031	1-23-42	84	House painter
0032	5-28-42	89	Janitor
0040	9-2-43	105	Operative
0041	9-7-43	100	Truck Driver
0042	5-9-43	104	Stock handler
0060	4-27-43	90	Operative
0061	4-25-43	90	Oiler
0062	4-1-43	90	Operative
0070	5-5-43	92	Operative
0071	7-6-42	97	Operative
0072	4-29-43	95	Operative
0080	7-26-43	110	Truck driver
0081	9-27-43	114	Truck driver
0082	10-15-42	106	Cab driver
0090	10-31-41	110	Bookkeeper
0091	5-6-42	100	Storekeeper
0092	7-26-42	106	Storekeeper
0100	8-7-44	108	Repairman
0101	8-7-44	114	Repairman
0102	9-10-44	111	Repairman
0110	1-22-43	101	Concessionaire
0111	6-10-43	102	Restaurateur
0112	6-17-43	97	Gas station owner
0120	6-25-42	104	Operative
0121	4-15-42	110	Operative
0122	7-20-42	106	Truck driver
0130	6-3-41	103	Plant superintendent
0131	4-1-41	108	Suggestion supervisor
0132	3-31-42	102	Fire Dept. Battalion Chief
0140	10-16-44	98	Postal superintendent
0141	10-21-44	98	Service manager
0142	7-21-44	103	Sales manager

1. Code numbers ending in 0 are non-delinquents; in 1, sometime delinquents; and in 2, repeated delinquents.

Code	Birthdate	I.Q.	Father's Occupation
0150	5-18-42	113	Engineer
0151	3-1-43	111	Industrial engineer
0152	7-3-41	111	Electrical engineer
0160	5-12-42	96	Set-up man
0161	3-14-42	93	Die sinker
0162	12-2-41	93	Mechanic
0170	7-12-43	100	Operative
0171	6-24-43	95	Railroad yard master
0172	7-17-43	94	Operative (M)[1]
0180	3-11-42	92	Set-up man
0181	8-15-41	89	Stock man
0182	4-9-42	99	Stock man
0190	10-30-42	107	Salesman
0191	4-14-42	100	Sales manager
0192	12-9-41	99	Salesman
0200	9-6-43	101	Operative
0201	12-16-43	109	Operative (M)
0202	2-22-43	102	Operative
0210	7-27-42	86	Operative
0211	10-13-42	85	Printer
0212	7-1-43	81	Operative
0220	9-9-42	106	Insurance agency owner
0221	10-17-41	111	Caterer
0222	12-23-41	109	Chain drugstore owner
0230	1-15-44	111	Operative
0231	7-24-45	107	Packer
0232	12-18-44	104	Laborer
0240	11-25-41	109	Repairman
0241	1-16-42	99	Repairman
0242	2-16-41	104	Repairman
0250	12-3-41	107	Repairman
0251	11-18-41	106	Spot welder
0252	7-13-41	107	Tool and die maker
0260	7-29-44	107	Tinsmith
0261	1-21-45	105	Inspector
0262	8-9-44	115	Trimmer

---

1. Mother's occupation; no father present.

Code	Birthdate	I.Q.	Father's Occupation
0270	3-1-42	88	Operative
0271	6-19-41	83	Operative
0272	2-13-42	87	Operative
0280	3-18-42	102	Welder
0281	10-21-42	103	Millwright
0282	7-15-42	105	Welder
0290	7-18-41	98	Operative
0291	7-13-42	107	Stenotypist
0292	2-19-42	101	Die maker
0300	8-13-42	101	Utility repairman
0301	7-29-42	101	Operative
0302	10-2-41	96	Furnace repairman
0310	1-30-41	104	Suggestion supervisor
0311	8-8-41	104	Shift superintendent
0312	7-18-41	102	Department supervisor
0320	7-15-42	107	Master mechanic
0321	2-2-42	104	Factory policeman
0322	2-7-42	97	Plant maintenance
0330	8-23-42	108	Truck driver
0331	5-21-42	110	Operative
0332	6-9-42	107	Operative
0340	9-4-43	93	Inspector
0341	7-30-44	99	Millwright
0342	9-2-44	94	Inspector
0360	4-26-41	116	Die designer
0361	4-23-42	121	Tool and die maker
0362	1-31-42	122	Process engineer
0370	10-25-44	110	Minister
0371	11-30-44	104	Store manager
0372	4-16-45	105	Attorney
0380	6-9-44	103	Inspector
0381	9-24-44	107	Operative
0382	10-24-44	102	Operative (M)
0390	8-31-42	114	Owner—small production shop
0391	11-19-41	109	Owner—appliance sales, serv.
0392	5-8-42	119	Owner—appliance sales, serv.
0400	8-9-43	99	Electrical repairman
0401	1-14-43	89	Machinist
0402	5-9-42	93	Welder

Code	Birthdate	I.Q.	Father's Occupation
0410	2-14-43	93	Carpenter
0411	7-13-43	98	Millwright
0412	11-12-43	95	Tinsmith
0420	3-21-43	97	Operative
0421	6-3-43	97	Operative
0422	9-1-43	100	Operative
0440	3-7-43	93	Mechanic
0441	9-22-42	93	Electrician
0442	6-21-43	89	Operative (M)
0450	12-18-42	126	Operative (M)
0451	8-13-42	120	Waitress (M)
0452	10-19-42	124	Operative
0470	12-3-41	95	Teacher
0471	10-25-41	104	Packaging engineer
0472	4-19-42	97	Products designer
0500	9-20-44	95	Tool repairman
0501	11-27-44	95	Millwright
0502	10-30-44	100	Serviceman
0510	5-22-43	102	Operative
0512	4-14-43	112	Operative (M)
0520	1-2-43	103	Inspector
0522	4-7-42	106	Inspector
0530	3-11-41	89	Sales clerk (M)
0532	3-2-41	89	Mailman
0540	7-20-41	97	Stockman
0542	6-20-42	95	Stockman
0550	1-21-44	87	Operative
0552	4-19-43	85	Operative
0560	8-19-41	100	Truck driver
0562	11-3-41	96	Foreman
0570	9-16-41	91	Operative
0572	2-6-42	90	Park tree man
0580	5-26-41	103	Tool and die worker
0582	2-17-42	102	Welder
0590	4-24-42	91	Factory clerk
0592	9-13-42	84	Sweeper

Code	Birthdate	I.Q.	Father's Occupation
0600	1-7-43	112	Operative
0602	5-21-43	112	Inspector
0610	4-3-41	101	Teacher (M)
0612	1-27-41	101	Metallurgical engineer
0620	11-2-41	106	Foreman
0622	7-10-41	102	Foreman
0630	1-9-44	87	Truck driver
0632	1-28-43	81	Operative
0640	3-24-41	101	Operative
0642	2-7-41	100	Operative (M)
0660	12-10-41	119	Plant protection
0662	2-12-41	109	Policeman
0670	11-16-41	105	Operative
0672	10-17-41	105	Factory clerk
0680	9-19-43	121	Operative
0682	10-31-43	128	Foreman
0690	1-26-42	95	Foreman
0692	6-13-41	95	Factory clerk
0700	10-17-45	93	Manager
0702	4-19-46	94	Accountant
0710	9-22-41	107	Operative
0712	5-20-42	108	Inspector
0720	7-18-42	87	Operative
0722	1-1-42	83	Factory clerk
0730	4-25-43	123	Plant maintenance
0732	5-31-43	122	Operative (M)
0750	7-29-41	115	Print shop owner
0752	6-3-41	106	Restaurateur
0760	10-6-41	105	Coin machine owner
0762	1-14-42	104	Bakery owner
0770	3-10-42	115	Policeman
0772	8-28-43	121	Bartender
0780	8-10-43	100	Operative
0782	9-13-43	102	Operative
0790	10-14-42	115	Factory clerk
0792	11-14-41	125	Store clerk

Code	Birthdate	I.Q.	Father's Occupation
0800	5-1-41	104	Truck driver
0802	6-29-41	104	Truck driver
0810	6-5-43	89	T.V. antenna installer
0812	6-23-42	81	Operative
0820	1-27-43	100	Mechanic
0822	5-26-43	90	Operative
0830	10-22-42	80	Factory clerk
0832	3-7-42	80	Factory maintenance
8040	12-6-42	94	Welder
0842	6-16-42	95	Inspector
0850	6-24-42	93	Operative
0852	4-22-43	96	Operative
0860	7-17-41	103	Truck driver
0862	5-26-41	107	Factory repairman
0870	5-25-43	106	Factory repairman
0872	8-30-42	116	Operative
0880	1-13-44	109	Tinsmith
0882	5-30-44	116	Operative
0890	3-22-42	82	Store maintenance
0892	6-25-43	89	Unemployed (M)
0900	1-5-42	104	Store manager
0902	4-26-42	95	Store manager
0910	8-17-43	108	Plant policeman
0912	5-5-44	109	Fireman
0920	10-14-41	99	Driver salesman
0922	6-27-41	102	Machine repairman
0930	12-16-42	89	Operative
0932	6-10-42	93	Foreman
0940	10-25-43	101	Truck driver
0942	3-16-43	102	Factory maintenance
0950	9-17-42	122	Elevator repairman
0952	4-15-42	120	Apprentice die maker
0960	10-30-41	91	City fire inspector
0962	7-3-42	85	Foreman
0970	2-5-42	106	Bricklayer
0972	5-2-42	105	Millwright

Code	Birthdate	I.Q.	Father's Occupation
0980	2-10-41	97	Stock manager
0982	3-13-41	95	Operative
0990	5-31-44	109	Gas station attendant
0992	3-30-44	103	Gas station attendant
1000	9-11-43	101	Railroad switchman
1002	6-13-43	109	Operative
1010	5-10-42	104	Machine repairman
1012	5-14-41	103	Operative
1020	6-25-42	105	Roller rink owner
1022	9-26-42	108	Restaurateur

APPENDIX II

SELECTED TABLES

Table A-1

A description of the core sample.

Social Status	Repeated Delinquents			Sometimes Delinquents			Non-Delinquents		
	Boys	Moth-ers	Fa-thers	Boys	Moth-ers	Fa-thers	Boys	Moth-ers	Fa-thers
White collar	20	19	16	10	10	9	20	18	18
Skilled	27	26	24	16	16	13	27	23	22
Unskilled	46	44	40	17	15	15	46	41	37
Total	93	89	80	43	41	37	93	82	77

Table A-2

Comparison of annual income among the families of delinquent and non-delinquent boys in the core sample (as
reported by question 62 [fathers]—What was your total
family income in 1957?).

Item	Under $5,000 (per cent)	$5,000-$6,999 (per cent)	$7,000-$9,999 (per cent)	More Than $10,000 (per cent)	? (per cent)	Total Per Cent	N
Repeated delin-quents	27	28	18	24	3	100	80
Sometime de-linquents	8	41	23	25	3	100	37
Non-delin-quents	17	36	31	15	1	100	77

Table A-3

Comparison of education level achieved by parents of delinquent and non-delinquent boys in the core sample (as
reported by question 58 [parents]—What was the highest
grade of school you completed?).

Item	Grade School or Less (per cent)	Some High School (per cent)	High School (per cent)	Beyond High School (per cent)	Total Per Cent	N
		Fathers				
Repeated delinquents	33	25	26	16	100	80
Sometime delinquents	35	16	41	8	100	37
Non-delinquents	32	30	29	9	100	77
		Mothers				
Repeated delinquents	27	43	20	10	100	89
Sometime delinquents	21	34	35	10	101	41
Non-delinquents	17	35	40	8	100	82

Table A-4

Comparison of place of origin of parents of delinquent and non-delinquent boys in the core sample (as reported by questions 59 and 60 [parents]—Did you grow up on a farm, in a small town, or city, or what? Where was this?).

Item	Rural Home (per cent)	Small Town (per cent)	Medium-sized Community (per cent)
Fathers			
Repeated delinquents	34	38	5
Sometime delinquents	24	24	3
Non-delinquents	39	19	6
Mothers			
Repeated delinquents	34	32	6
Sometime delinquents	22	32	2
Non-delinquents	36	28	2

Item	Flint (per cent)	Else-where in Mich. (per cent)	Midwest (per cent)	West (per cent)
Fathers				
Repeated delinquents	18	35	24	--
Sometime delinquents	24	41	13	--
Non-delinquents	23	33	16	--
Mothers				
Repeated delinquents	22	34	23	1
Sometime delinquents	24	44	17	5
Non-delinquents	20	40	22	--

Table A-4 (Continued)

Large City and Suburbs (per cent)	? (per cent)	Total Per Cent	N
Fathers			
21	3	100	80
49	--	100	37
36	--	100	77
Mothers			
25	2	100	89
44	--	100	41
34	--	100	82

Northeast and Atlantic (per cent)	South (per cent)	Foreign (per cent)	? (per cent)	Total Per Cent	N
Fathers					
4	13	4	1	99	80
--	19	--	3	100	37
4	16	5	3	100	77
Mothers					
5	14	1	--	100	89
--	7	--	2	99	41
2	14	1	--	99	82

Table A-5

The higher the socio-economic status of a school district, the better its recreational facilities tend to be.

Socio-economic Status Indices	Recreational Indices		
	Land Allotment	Land Use	General
Average value of d.u.'s	.04[a] (.32)	.27 (.02)	.25 (.02)
Per cent owners	.40 (<.0007)	.007 (.48)	.20 (.06)
Weighted value	.35 (.003)	.19 (.07)	.37 (.002)

a. Entries are Kendall's rank-order coefficient, τ (and their one-tailed probability levels).

Table A-6

Correlations of boys', mothers', and fathers' judgments
of the power relations between fathers and mothers were
from low to moderately positive; greater covariation was
present in the families of non-delinquents.

	Repeated Delinquents			Non-Delinquents		
	r	N	p-level (2t)	r	N	p-level (2t)
Boys and mothers	.16	55	<.10	.56	63	<.0005
Boys and fathers	.29	69	<.01	.38	74	<.0005
Mothers and fathers	.25	50	<.05	.44	57	<.0005

Table A-7

Parents of repeated delinquents do not differ much from the parents of non-delinquents in the kinds of occupations they would like their sons to enter.

Question 32: What kind of a job would you like (your son) to have as an adult?

	Professional, Technical; Kindred (1)	Self-Employed Businessmen; Artisans (2)	Managers; Officials (3)
Fathers			
White collar			
Repeated delinquents	35%	6%	--%
Non-delinquents	38	--	13
Skilled			
Repeated delinquents	45	--	5
Non-delinquents	54	--	--
Unskilled			
Repeated delinquents	26	3	--
Non-delinquents	35	--	--
Total			
Repeated delinquents	34	3	1
Non-delinquents	41	--	3

	White Collar		Skilled	
	Repeaters	Non-del.	Repeaters	Non-del.
Mean	2.2	1.2	2.1	1.4
N	10		14	
t	1.6		1.7	
p	<.05		<.05	

Table A-7 (Continued)

Cleri-cal; Sales (4)	Crafts-men; Fore-men (5)	Opera-tives; Kin-dred (6)	Un-skilled Labor-ers (7)	Other	?	N
		Fathers				
--%	--%	--%	--%	6%	53%	17
6	--	--	--	--	44	16
5	14	--	--	--	32	22
--	13	4	--	4	25	24
8	11	5	--	3	45	38
3	18	--	--	--	45	40
5	9	3	--	3	43	77
3	13	1	--	1	39	80

	Unskilled		Total	
	Repeaters	Non-del.	Repeaters	Non-del.
Mean	1.5	2.3	1.9	1.8
N	20		44	
t	1.0		0.2	
p	NR		NR	

Table A-7 (Continued)

	Profes-sional, Tech-nical; Kindred (1)	Self-Employed Business-men; Artisans (2)	Man-agers; Officials (3)
	Mothers		
White collar			
Repeated delinquents	28%	11%	--%
Non-delinquents	53	--	--
Skilled			
Repeated delinquents	35	9	--
Non-delinquents	54	4	--
Unskilled			
Repeated delinquents	34	--	--
Non-delinquents	43	--	3
Total			
Repeated delinquents	33	5	--
Non-delinquents	48	1	1

	White Collar		Skilled	
	Repeaters	Non-del.	Repeaters	Non-del.
Mean	1.3	1.3	1.9	1.5
N	6		22	
t	--		0.7	
p	NR		NR	

Table A-7 (Continued)

Cler- ical; Sales (4)	Crafts- men; Fore- men (5)	Opera- tives; Kin- dred (6)	Un- skilled Labor- ers (7)	Other	?	N
		Mothers				
--%	11%	--%	--%	--%	50%	18
5	--	--	--	--	42	19
9	4	--	--	9	35	23
--	4	--	--	--	38	26
5	5	7	--	--	50	44
--	10	--	--	3	43	40
5	6	4	--	2	46	85
--	6	--	--	1	41	85

	Unskilled		Total	
	Repeaters	Non-del.	Repeaters	Non-del.
Mean	2.3	2.3	2.0	1.8
N	20		48	
t	--		0.5	
p	NR		NR	

Table A-8

Correlations show that the higher the school average a boy achieved in the seventh grade, the higher his occupational aspirations and his parents' aspirations for him tend to be.

	Fathers' Report			Mothers' Report			Boys' Report		
	r	N	p-level	r	N	p-level	r	N	p-level
White collar									
Repeated delinquents	.08	5		.90	6		.72	11	
Non-delinquents	.68	7		.39	10		.03	17	
Skilled									
Repeated delinquents	.25	14		.26	10		.32	21	
Non-delinquents	.15	16		.47	13		.31	23	
Unskilled									
Repeated delinquents	.64	17		.68	19		.19	36	
Non-delinquents	.26	21		.48	20		.45	40	
Total									
Repeated delinquents	.41	36	<.01	.60	35	<.0005	.32	68	<.005
Non-delinquents	.29	44	<.05	.46	43	<.005	.32	80	<.005

Table A-9

The higher the school average a boy achieved in the seventh grade, the better he views his chances of getting the job he wants, except among the white collar repeated delinquents.

	r	N	p-level
White collar			
Repeated delinquents	-.27	11	
Non-delinquents	.23	17	
Skilled			
Repeated delinquents	.31	21	
Non-delinquents	.19	23	
Unskilled			
Repeated delinquents	.31	38	
Non-delinquents	.23	39	
Total			
Repeated delinquents	.30	70	<.01
Non-delinquents	.22	79	<.05

Table A-10

Repeated delinquents aspire to hold less prestigeful occupations than matched non-delinquents.

Question 25: What job would you like to have when you
take a job?

	Profes-sional, Tech-nical; Kindred (1)	Self-Employed Business-men; Artisans (2)	Man-agers; Officials (3)
White collar			
Repeated delinquents	20%	15%	5%
Non-delinquents	55	--	5
Skilled			
Repeated delinquents	30	4	--
Non-delinquents	48	--	4
Unskilled			
Repeated delinquents	24	4	4
Non-delinquents	41	2	--
Total			
Repeated delinquents	25	6	3
Non-delinquents	46	1	2

	White Collar		Skilled	
	Repeaters	Non-del.	Repeaters	Non-del.
Mean	3.6	2.7	3.4	2.8
N	15		21	
t	1.4		1.1	
p	<.05		NR	

Table A-10 (Continued)

Clerical; Sales (4)	Craftsmen; Foremen (5)	Operatives; Kindred (6)	Unskilled Laborers (7)	Other	?	N
--%	25%	--%	5%	10%	20%	20
10	5	5	10	--	10	20
4	33	7	--	11	11	27
--	26	4	4	7	7	27
--	30	22	2	4	17	46
--	28	9	--	13	7	46
1	30	13	2	8	12	93
2	23	6	3	9	8	93

	Unskilled		Total	
	Repeaters	Non-del.	Repeaters	Non-del.
Mean	4.1	3.2	3.8	3.0
N	40		76	
t	2.2		2.8	
p	<.01		<.003	

Table A-11

Delinquents and non-delinquents tend to rank jobs by quality in the same way, and both agree with the rankings
made by a national sample of people.

Question 19 (questionnaire): Please rate each job on how
good you think it is generally. You may or
may not want any of the jobs yourself, but
you can still rate it on how good a job you
think it is.

	Judge	Chemi-cal En-gineer	Adver-tising Execu-tive	Factory Man-ager
White collar				
Repeated delinquents	8%	1%	4%	6.5%
Non-delinquents	2	1	4	5
			$\tau = .58$; $p = .004$ (1t)	
Skilled				
Repeated delinquents	8	1	3	3
Non-delinquents	3	1	4.5	6
			$\tau = .66$; $p = .001$ (2t)	
Unskilled				
Repeated delinquents	7	1	4	3
Non-delinquents	2	1	5	3
			$\tau = .76$; $p = .002$ (2t)	
Total				
Repeated delinquents	6	2	4	9.5
Non-delinquents	2	1	4	8.5
			$\tau = .65$; $p = .001$ (2t)	
Warner rankings	1.5	1.5	4.5	3

	White Collar		Skilled	
	Repeaters	Non-del.	Repeaters	Non-del.
τ with Warner ranks	.52	.69	.69	.70
p-level (2t)	.01	.001	.001	.001

Table A-11 (Continued)

Real Estate Sales-man	Office Man-ager	Book-keeper	Spot Welder	TV Re-pair-man	Store Clerk	Assem-bly Line Worker	Waiter
4%	2%	6.5%	9%	4%	10%	11%	12%
6	3	9	11	7	8	12	10
5	3	6.5	9	6.5	10	11	12
7	2	8	9	4.5	10	11.5	11.5
5	2	9	8	6	10	11	12
7	4	8	9	6	10	11	12
1	3	7	8	5	9.5	11	12
6	3	7	10	5	8.5	12	11
4.5	6	7	8	9.5	9.5	11.5	11.5

Unskilled		Total	
Repeaters	Non-del.	Repeaters	Non-del.
.66	.91	.70	.61
.001	.0001	.0001	.002

LIST OF REFERENCES

LIST OF REFERENCES

Aichhorn, A. *Wayward youth.* New York: Viking Press, 1935.

Back, K. W. Influence through social communication. *J. abnorm. Psychol.,* 1951, 46, 9-23.

Bandura, A., and Walters, R. H. *Adolescent Aggression*—A Study of the Influence of Child-Training Practices and Family Interrelationships. Copyright ⓒ The Ronald Press Company, New York, 1959.

Blalock, H. M. *Social statistics.* New York: McGraw-Hill, 1960.

Bordua, D. J. Delinquency theory and research in the United States: major trends since 1920. *Kaelner Zeitschrift,* 1957.

_____. Juvenile delinquency and "anomie": an attempt at replication. *Social Problems,* 1959, 6, 230-258.

Bronfenbrenner, U. Some familial antecedents of responsibility and leadership in adolescents. In B. M. Bass (Ed.), *Studies in leadership.* New York: Henry Holt, in press.

Burgess, E. W. The economic factor in juvenile delinquency. *J. crim. Law, Criminol., and polit. Sci.,* 1952, 43 (1), 29-42.

Burgess, E. W., and Locke, H. J. *The family, from institution to companionship.* New York: American Book Co., 1945.

Carr, L. J. *Delinquency control.* New York: Harper, 1950.

Cartwright, D. Achieving change in people: some applications of group dynamics theory. *Hum. Relat.,* 1951, 4, 381-392.

Cohen, A. K. *Delinquent boys.* Chicago: The Free Press, 1955.

_____. Middle-class delinquency and the social structure. Address to the Amer. Sociol. Ass., Chicago, September, 1957.

Durkheim, E. *Suicide.* (transl.) Chicago: The Free Press, 1951.

Faris, R. E. L. Ecological factors in human behavior. In J. V. McHunt (Ed.), *Personality and the behavior disorders.* Vol. 2. New York: Ronald Press, 1944. Pp. 736-757.

Festinger, L., Schachter, S., and Back, K. W. *Social pressure in informal groups: a study of human factors in housing.* New York: Harper, 1950.

French, J. R. P., Jr., and Raven, B. The bases of social power. In D. Cartwright, *Studies in social power.* Ann Arbor, Mich.: Institute for Social Research, 1959. Pp. 150-167.

Glaser, D., and Rice, K. Crime, age and employment. *Amer. sociol. Rev.*, 1959, 24, 679-686.

Glueck, S., and Glueck, Eleanor. *Unravelling juvenile delinquency.* Cambridge, Mass.: Harvard Univer. Press, 1950.

Gold, M. Punishment, guilt, and behavior in school. Ann Arbor, Mich.: Institute for Social Research, 1958. (Mimeo.)

Gold, M., and Slater, C. Office, factory, store—and family: a study of integration setting. *Amer. sociol. Rev.*, 1958, 23, 64-74.

Grunes, W. F. On perception of occupations. *Personnel and Guidance J.*, 1956, 34, 276-279.

Healy, W., and Bronner, A. *New light on delinquency and its treatment.* New Haven: Yale Univer. Press, 1936.

Hewitt, L. E., and Jenkins, R. L. *Fundamental patterns of maladjustment.* Springfield, Ill.: State Printing Office, 1946.

Hoffman, L. W. Effects of maternal employment on the child. *Child Development*, 1961, 32, 187-197.

Hollingshead, A. B. *Elmtown's youth.* New York: Wiley, 1949.

_____. Class differences in family stability. *Ann. Amer. Acad. polit. soc. Sci.*, 1950, 272, 39-46.

Kersten, L. A study of recreational opportunity among different social and economic classes in the city of Flint, Michigan. Unpublished manuscript, Social Science Research Project, Univer. of Michigan, 1958.

Kobrin, S. The conflict of values in delinquency areas. *Amer. sociol. Rev.*, 1951, 16, 653-661.

Komarovsky, M. *The unemployed man and his family.* New York: Dryden Press, 1940.

Kvaraceus, W. C. Juvenile delinquency and social class. *J. educ. Sociol.*, 1944, 18, 51-54.

_____. Juvenile delinquency and the school. Yonkers, N. Y.: World Book Co., 1945.

Kvaraceus, W. C., and Miller, W. B. (Eds.). *Delinquent behavior: culture and the individual.* Washington, D. C.: National Educ. Ass., 1959.

Laird, M. S. *Annual report for the years 1931-1932.* Cuyahoga County (Cleveland) Juvenile Court, 1933.

Lander, B. *Towards an understanding of juvenile delinquency.* New York: Columbia Univer. Press, 1954.

Lasswell, H. D. *The analysis of political behavior.* New York: Oxford Univer. Press, 1948.

Lewin, K. *Field theory in social science.* New York: Harper, 1951.

McClelland, D. C., Atkinson, J., Clark, R., and Lowell, E. *The achievement motive.* New York: Appleton-Century-Crofts, 1953.

McCord, J., and McCord, W. The effects of parental role model on criminality. *J. soc. Issues,* 1958, 14 (3), 66-75.

McGrath, J. E. A study of phenomenal resolution of experimentally induced strain in cognitive structures. Unpublished doctoral dissertation, Univer. of Michigan, 1955.

Merrill, M. A. *Problems of child delinquency.* New York: Houghton Mifflin, 1947.

Merton, R. K. Social structure and anomie. *Amer. sociol. Rev.,* 1958, 3, 672-682.

Miller, D. R., and Swanson, G. E. *The changing American parent.* New York: Wiley, 1958.

_____. *Inner conflict and defense.* New York: Henry Holt, 1960.

Myers, J. K., and Roberts, B. H. *Family and class dynamics in mental illness.* New York: Wiley, 1959.

Neumeyer, M. H. *Juvenile delinquency in modern society.* New York: Van Nostrand, 1949.

Newcomb, T. M. *Personality and social change: attitude formation in a student community.* New York: Dryden Press, 1943.

Nye, F. I. *Family relationships and delinquent behavior.* New York: Wiley, 1958.

Parsons, T., and Bales, R. F. *Family.* Chicago: The Free Press, 1955.

Pope, L. *Millhands and preachers.* New Haven: Yale Univer. Press, 1942.

Reckless, W., Dinitz, S., and Kay, B. The self component in potential delinquency. *Amer. sociol. Rev.,* 1957, 22, 566, 570.

Redl, F., and Wineman, D. *The aggressive child.* Chicago: The Free Press, 1957.

Reineman, J. Juvenile delinquency in Philadelphia and economic trends. *Temple Univer. Law Quart.,* 1947, 20, 7.

Reiss, A. J., Jr. Delinquency as a failure of personal and social controls. *Amer. sociol. Rev.,* 1951, 16, 196-207.

_____. Educational achievement norms, aspirations, and conforming behavior. Address to Univer. of Michigan Dept. Sociol., Ann Arbor, May, 1959.

Scagnelli, J. Facts about adolescent members in Boys Clubs. Boys Clubs of America, 1960. (Mimeo.)

Sexton, P. C. Social class in a big city school system. Unpublished doctoral dissertation, Wayne State Univer., 1960.

Shanas, E. *Recreation and delinquency.* Chicago: Univer. of Chicago Press, 1942.

Shaw, C. R., and McKay, H. D. *Juvenile delinquency and urban areas.* Chicago: Univer. of Chicago Press, 1942.

Shaw, D. C. The relationship of socio-economic status to educational achievement in grades IV to VIII. *J. educ. Res.,* 1943, 7, 197-210.

Siegel, S. *Non-parametric statistics.* New York: McGraw-Hill, 1956.

Solomon, D. Influences on the decisions of adolescents. Unpublished doctoral dissertation, Univer. of Michigan, 1960.

Stermer, J. E. *Report to Judge D. J. Healy, Jr., Wayne County Juvenile Court* (Detroit), 1936.

Sutherland, E. H. *Principles of criminology.* New York: Lippincott, 1939.

_____. Address to Ohio Valley Sociol. Soc., 1942. Reported in A. K. Cohen, A. Lindesmith, and K. Schuessler (Eds.), *The Sutherland papers.* Bloomington, Ind.: Indiana Univer. Press, 1956.

Tappan, P. W. *Juvenile delinquency.* New York: McGraw-Hill, 1949.

Thomas, W. I. *The unadjusted girl.* Boston: Little, Brown, 1937.

Thrasher, F. M. The Boys Club and juvenile delinquency. *Amer. J. Sociol.,* 1936, July, 66-80.

Warner, W. L., Havighurst, R. J., and Loeb, M. B. *Who shall be educated?* New York: Harper, 1944.

Warner, W. L., Meeker, M., and Eels, K. *Social class in America.* Chicago: Science Res. Associates, 1949.

Wattenberg, W. W. *Boy repeaters.* Detroit: Wayne State Univer. Press, 1947.

Whyte, W. F. *Street corner society.* Chicago: Univer. of Chicago Press, 1943.

INDEX

PUBLICATIONS OF THE

INSTITUTE FOR SOCIAL RESEARCH

These publications may be obtained from the
    Librarian
    Institute for Social Research
    The University of Michigan
    Ann Arbor, Michigan

Research Center for Group Dynamics Series
    RCGD No. 1   Cnanging Attitudes Through Social Contact
                 by Leon Festinger, Harold H. Kelley

    RCGD No. 2   Graph Theory As A Mathematical Model in Social
                 Science
                 by Frank Harary, Robert Z. Norman

    RCGD No. 3   Measuring Group Cohesiveness
                 by Lester M. Libo

    RCGD No. 4   Learning Across Cultures
                 by Jeanne Watson, Ronald Lippitt

    RCGD No. 5   Role Relations in the Mental Health Professions
                 by Alvin Zander, Arthur R. Cohen, Ezra Stotland

    RCGD No. 6   Studies in Social Power by Dorwin Cartwright

Survey Research Center Series
    SRC No. 1   Public Use of the Library
                 by Angus Campbell, Cnarles A. Metzner

    SRC No. 2   Productivity, Supervision and Morale In An Office
                 Situation
                 by Daniel Katz, Nathan Maccoby, Nancy C. Morse

    SRC No. 4   Industrial Mobility in Michigan
                 by George Katona, James N. Morgan

    SRC No. 5   Productivity, Supervision and Morale Among Rail-
                 road Workers
                 by Daniel Katz, Nathan Maccoby, Gerald Gurin,
                 Lucretia G. Floor

    SRC No. 6   Big Business As the People See It
                 by Burton R. Fisher, Stephen B. Withey

SRC No. 9 The People Elect a President
            by Angus Campbell, Robert L. Kahn

SRC No. 10 Satisfactions In The White-Collar Job
            by Nancy Morse

SRC No. 12 Consumer Attitudes and Demands, 1950-1952
            by George Katona, Eva Mueller

SRC No. 14 Group Cohesiveness In The Industrial Work Group
            by Stanley E. Seashore

SRC No. 15 Group Differences In Attitudes and Votes
            by Angus Campbell, Homer C. Cooper

SRC No. 16 Consumer Expectations, 1953-1956
            by George Katona, Eva Mueller

SRC No. 17 Processes of Organization
            by Robert Weiss

Research Center for Group Dynamics Series
Publication No. 7